uittard GUITTARD Guittard's Guittard GUITTARD Guittard
uittard GUITTARD MFG. CO. Guittard Guittard GUITTARD MFG. CO. Guittar
uittard GUITTARD Guittard's Guittard GUITTARD Guittard
uittard GUITTARD MFG. CO. Guittard Guittard GUITTARD MFG. CO. Guittar
uittard GUITTARD Guittard's Guittard GUITTARD Guittard
uittard GUITTARD MFG. CO. Guittard Guittard GUITTARD MFG. CO. Guittar
uittard GUITTARD Guittard's Guittard GUITTARD Guittard
uittard GUITTARD MFG. CO. Guittard Guittard GUITTARD MFG. CO. Guittar
uittard GUITTARD Guittard's Guittard GUITTARD Guittard
uittard GUITTARD MFG. CO. Guittard Guittard GUITTARD MFG. CO. Guittar
uittard GUITTARD Guittard's Guittard GUITTARD Guittard
uittard GUITTARD MFG. CO. Guittard Guittard GUITTARD MFG. CO. Guittar
uittard GUITTARD Guittard's Guittard GUITTARD Guittard
uittard GUITTARD MFG. CO. Guittard Guittard GUITTARD MFG. CO. Guittar
uittard GUITTARD Guittard's Guittard GUITTARD Guittard
uittard GUITTARD MFG. CO. Guittard Guittard GUITTARD MFG. CO. Guittar
uittard GUITTARD Guittard's Guittard GUITTARD Guittard
uittard GUITTARD MFG. CO. Guittard Guittard GUITTARD MFG. CO. Guittar

uittard GUITTARD Guittard's Guittard GUITTARD Guittar

uittard GUITTARD MFG. CO. Guittard Guittard GUITTARD MFG. CO. Guitta

uittard GUITTARD Guittard's Guittard GUITTARD Guittar

uittard GUITTARD MFG. CO. Guittard Guittard GUITTARD MFG. CO. Guitta

uittard GUITTARD Guittard's Guittard GUITTARD Guittar

uittard GUITTARD MFG. CO. Guittard Guittard GUITTARD MFG. CO. Guitta

uittard GUITTARD Guittard's Guittard GUITTARD Guittar

uittard GUITTARD MFG. CO. Guittard Guittard GUITTARD MFG. CO. Guitta

uittard GUITTARD Guittard's Guittard GUITTARD Guittar

uittard GUITTARD MFG. CO. Guittard Guittard GUITTARD MFG. CO. Guitta

uittard GUITTARD Guittard's Guittard GUITTARD Guittar

uittard GUITTARD MFG. CO. Guittard Guittard GUITTARD MFG. CO. Guitta

uittard GUITTARD Guittard's Guittard GUITTARD Guittar

uittard GUITTARD MFG. CO. Guittard Guittard GUITTARD MFG. CO. Guitta

uittard GUITTARD Guittard's Guittard GUITTARD Guittar

uittard GUITTARD MFG. CO. Guittard Guittard GUITTARD MFG. CO. Guitta

uittard GUITTARD Guittard's Guittard GUITTARD Guittar

uittard GUITTARD MFG. CO. Guittard Guittard GUITTARD MFG. CO. Guitta

# Guittard®

## CHOCOLATE COOKBOOK

Decadent Recipes from San Francisco's
Premium Bean-to-Bar Chocolate Company

AMY GUITTARD

FOREWORD BY
ALICE MEDRICH

Photographs by
ANTONIS ACHILLEOS

CHRONICLE BOOKS
SAN FRANCISCO

Library of Congress Cataloging-in-Publication Data available.
ISBN 978-1-4521-3533-5

Manufactured in China

MIX
Paper from
responsible sources
FSC™ C008047
www.fsc.org

Designed by Vanessa Dina
Prop styling by Christine Wolheim
Food styling by Lillian Kang
Typesetting by DC Type

10 9 8 7 6 5 4 3 2 1

Chronicle Books LLC
680 Second Street
San Francisco, California 94107
www.chroniclebooks.com

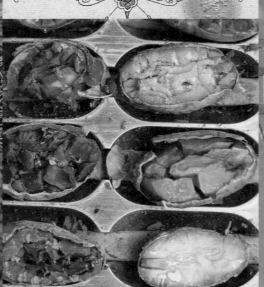

# Contents
•••••

# *Foreword*

There has never been a more exciting time for chocolate lovers and home bakers. The best supermarkets carry a dazzling array of chocolates for eating and baking. Even more choices can be found in specialty shops and online.

At a time when new chocolates made by an ever increasing number of small chocolate-makers seem to pop up every week, I love knowing that one family-owned company has been making superb chocolate in Northern California for about a century and a half. Guittard Chocolate is the oldest continuously family-owned American chocolate company; the fourth generation is at the helm today with a fifth generation rising.

Not too long ago, I sat with Guittard President Gary Guittard and Amy Guittard, his daughter and the company's marketing director. We were in his office to taste the first production batch of a brand-new baking line. It was an honor to be included in what was otherwise a very private meeting. I was immediately taken by the modern clean lines of the new packaging, its vibrant cacao-pod colors, and even the convenient detail of having three individually wrapped, easy-to-break-up, two-ounce bars in each box. But it was the chocolate itself that really made me smile. Guittard has an established reputation for Belgian- and French-style chocolate—beloved for its smooth, dark-roasted cocoa-y flavors, and probably the hero ingredient in some of your favorite desserts and confections. But this new line was part of Collection Etienne, single-origin and special-blend bars made more in the French than Belgian style, and so beautifully done. The chocolates were aromatic, complex, and bright with a pleasing range of flavors: deep and lingering base chocolate notes, a hint of tartness and cherry, a gentle acidity, and just enough astringency to carry the flavor forward. Sophisticated, juicy, and delicious. These were chocolates for an updated American palate, a chocolate-savvy modern home baker. I'm sure I smiled as I tasted. Each of the new chocolates, including the unsweetened 100% cacao bar, was a delicious nibble—not just good for baking! That tasting served to remind me that companies that thrive over five generations do not do so by sitting still. They continually create and evolve.

If you are a home baker mostly familiar with the iconic gold bag of Guittard chocolate chips, you may not be aware that the company also makes an enormous array of quality chocolate for professionals, and always has. Many of America's best bakers, pastry chefs, and confectioners have quietly and confidently used Guittard chocolate for years, even when others were using either lesser chocolate or big-name imports. Go ahead and do what I do: Ask the server in your favorite restaurant what kind of chocolate was used to make the fantastic chocolate dessert you just ate. You will likely learn that it was Guittard.

If you are a recent convert or ardent follower of artisan chocolates, you may not know that Guittard was the first (and still the only) established American company to launch an artisan line of single-origin and special-blend bars. It was the very beginning of a renaissance in American chocolate-making and a new era for chocolate consumers, too.

Prior to that time, there were no American-made and -marketed single-origin bars. With a single exception, American chocolates were not yet labeled with cacao percentages either. Traditional chocolate-makers were always protective about every detail of their process. Cacao blends and sources, cacao and cacao butter percentages, and methods and equipment were all considered trade secrets to be hidden from the public and from competitors. But that has changed. Today, every aspect of chocolate making is more transparent, from the plantation to the retail shelf; or as we say in the industry, from bean to bar. This new era of transparency has resulted in even greater interest and more passion for chocolate, and so many new self-proclaimed chocolate connoisseurs!

Guittard has helped shape this modern era of chocolate by playing an even greater leadership role in the industry than ever before. Gary frequently shares his knowledge and passion for chocolate in public forums. He spearheaded a successful fight to preserve the highest standards for chocolate, rather than allow non–cacao butter fats to be included within the definition of chocolate. The company works with global organizations to promote sustainability, collaboration, better prices for the farmers, and community education at the farm level, and to find and protect rare varieties of cacao. Guittard not only continues to make great chocolate that gets better and better, but Gary Guittard has become a respected and admired statesman and a valued role model and resource for emerging young chocolate-makers everywhere.

As a chocolate lover, pastry chef, and cookbook author myself, I'm honored to recognize Guittard's leadership and standard of excellence and I am thankful to Amy for telling the Guittard family story and sharing the family recipes from the generations that precede her.

Happy reading and *bon appétit*,

*Alice Medrich*

Despite growing up in a family of chocolate-makers in a city with a rich and revolutionary food history, I'm still surprised by the bounty of food-stuffs found in every San Francisco neighborhood. You'll happen upon heirloom tomato plants and wild blackberry bushes on a stroll through Buena Vista Park. You'll see rosemary growing in Potrero Hill and lavender near Coit Tower. New neighborhood restaurants appear each week, pushing the edges of the latest flavor pairings while the city's classics are regularly reinvented. Now more than ever, there's a high degree of curiosity regarding the faces and places behind our food. Add a daily chocolate fix to the mix and the culinary world offers endless delicious opportunities.

Enter the *Guittard Chocolate Cookbook.*

The kitchen is one of my favorite places in the house, especially when we're making something with chocolate and testing new recipes. As you might imagine, as the oldest continuously family-owned and -operated chocolate company in the United States, Guittard has amassed quite a collection of recipes through the years. Inspired by San Francisco's love of food and by my family's obsession with chocolate, I first considered writing a cookbook during the summer of my sophomore year in college. Some of our recipes had made guest appearances on the back of our retail baking-chip bags, and other family favorites were included in a basic staple-bound book with little more than an ingredient list and directions, yet there was still too much delicious storytelling left untold. And so, this became my summer project. But my cookbook-writing plans gave way to the lure of the Pacific, and I spent more time surfing that summer than I did in the kitchen.

Fast-forward to 2012. I had been working at the chocolate company for just a few months when I found my great-great-grandfather's formula book on my dad's desk—pages of Etienne's elegant calligraphy chronicling his original chocolate recipes. That book beautifully captured the essence of the company's history, creativity, and inspiration. After examining it, I realized I could make a modern-day version. Instead of listing the pounds of cacao beans purchased or the roasting temperatures, as he did, I could share the formulas of the sweet treats we grew up with; the very formulas I held in my hands—recipes that my family has developed and made from our own chocolate.

From the formulas Etienne brought from his uncle's factory in France, my great-great-grandfather, great-grandfather, grandfather, and now my father have continued to refine our chocolate-making techniques. As I leafed through the antique book, I realized just how much these legendary formulas influenced not only our business but also chocolate-making in the United States. Through the industrial age and all the growth San Francisco has seen, we've held on to what's made Guittard a singular company for a century and a half: Quality, exploration, tradition, and trust.

**The People Behind Guittard Chocolate**

Since our founding, we've developed a close-knit family of employees, customers, suppliers, and growers who give our chocolate its unique Guittard flavor. The innovative spirit and entrepreneurial mindset that led Etienne to carry chocolate from France to California is written into our family's DNA, pushing us to seek the best of the best. In fact, we're never quite satisfied—we're always looking to find new beans, make new blends, and try new methods.

For us, the artisan craft is all about the creative process, which allows us to celebrate not just the ingredients and steps that go into making chocolate but also the relationships created along the way. These treasured relationships mirror the individualities of the beans. The people who've worked beside us for many years are part of the story of our chocolate—from the farms to the factory. In some cases, three generations from one family have worked in our factory, and these people tie us to our roots on San Francisco's Main Street. Accountants who worked under the leadership of my grandfather, Horace A. Guittard ("Mr. G," as they called him), share their memories of him and of the roaster who manned the machines on Commercial Street, what the city looked like then, and how it's changed. Mark, our vice president of sales, sits at the same desk his father did, and my dad sits at the same desk my grandfather used. These traditions tell a story of my family, and they are part of a bigger story: the history of San Francisco's role in chocolate-making.

The story begins with my great-great-grandfather Etienne, who left Tournus, France, in the mid-1800s to come to Northern California in search of gold. With him he brought chocolate from his uncle's factory in France to get equipment and supplies to set up shop and sell in San Francisco. When he realized that he was able to get a pretty penny for those chocolate treats, he sailed back to France to get equipment and supplies to set up a factory. In 1868, he returned to San Francisco and opened Guittard Chocolate on Sansome Street, selling not only fine chocolate but also coffee, tea, and spices.

My great-grandfather Horace C. Guittard, Etienne's son, was at the helm when the 1906 earthquake destroyed much of San Francisco, including our Sansome Street factory. At that time, San Francisco was overflowing with different purveyors of commodities south of Market Street—from coffee to tea to chocolate—which were mostly family-owned businesses. These owners formed a tight-knit community of passionate crafters who cared about the success of our burgeoning city. The Brandenstein family, who owned MJB Coffee, jumped in to help us get back on our feet. After a brief stay on Commercial Street while we rebuilt the business, Horace eventually moved the factory to Main Street and focused on making chocolate.

Guittard Chocolate stayed on Main Street until the property had to be sold to the city to make room for the Embarcadero Freeway. In 1954, my grandfather moved the company twenty minutes south of San Francisco to Burlingame, where we are today—roasting and refining every cacao bean with even more care than the generation before. Gary, my dad and Etienne's great-grandson, is the current president of Guittard Chocolate Company.

Etienne brought into his chocolate-making tradition an attitude and a culture that continue within Guittard today. His curiosity, creativity, and yen for discovery inspired him to create a business focused on crafting a premium chocolate. Guittard was built on quality and on making a unique chocolate with its own distinctive flavor profile. We'd be the first to tell you that we're a bit obsessed with all that goes into making chocolate, especially when it comes to finding the best beans and using the finest ingredients.

Both the cacao beans we source as well as the process we've honed over the years affect the flavor of chocolate. The key has been to refine our process in a way that captures the inherent flavor characteristics of the cacao beans we use. Each type of bean we receive in San Francisco has its own flavor traits. The challenge—and one we take on with great pleasure—is to adapt our process to the different characteristics of each cacao varietal and origin. We're constantly refining our methods in a quest to bring to the bakers, confectioners, chocolate lovers, and artisans of the food world a world-class chocolate for their recipes.

Etienne's passionate dedication to chocolate-making has sparked every generation from Horace C. and then Horace A. to my late uncle Jay and my father, Gary. The fifth generation of Guittards—my cousin Clark, my brother, Jesse, and I—share our ancestors' passion for chocolate. As we carry on the family tradition, each member of my family takes pride in knowing that Etienne would approve of the chocolate we craft and the company we've become.

## Sourcing the Bean and Honoring the Farmer

Adding to the legacy of Master Chocolatiers that began in France, our family continues to produce extraordinary chocolate every step of the way—from bean sourcing and taste-testing to discovering and creating new products for customers and being a responsible industry leader. It all begins with really great cacao beans, and here's where I send a special note of thanks to my grandfather Horace A. (known to me as Popsi).

Popsi used to go on goodwill trips with what was then called the Chocolate Manufacturers Association. On those trips, he would meet with the cacao farmers to learn about their farming approaches and post-harvest techniques in an effort to buy the best beans in each region. While there's been a sudden resurgence in the chocolate industry to reconnect with individual farmers, not long ago many cacao bean buyers were moving away from an emphasis on origins in favor of consolidating their supply chains and traders. In large part because of Popsi, Guittard resisted this trend, choosing instead to keep buying directly from the farms we'd always sourced from and to process each batch of beans individually to bring out the best flavor. Today, we remain committed to the relationships Popsi formed with farmers. We value our connections with many of the same farms (now with a new generation of farmers) and cooperatives, all found on the trips my dad and I have taken to source new growers. Our relationships with farmers are a big part of what makes Guittard chocolate taste so good.

## Taste and Memory

Whenever we're experiencing chocolate, whether it's beans out of the roaster, the unsweetened chocolate that comes from the mills, the finished chocolate off the production lines, or a luscious, rich ganache made from our chocolate, my dad reminds us, "Taste has memory." He'll say it over and over again, and it never gets old because it's so very true. Think about the first chocolate you remember experiencing. You remember the flavor, right? Taste that same kind of chocolate bar years later, and if it's changed you'll notice. If it hasn't, you'll be taken back to the time you had your first bite. The flavors we perceive come not just from the textures and the smells we experience but also from a specific memory—the people, the place, the time—of that experience. We remember not just our first taste of chocolate as kids but moments, like the times my dad made hot chocolate for trips out to Candlestick Park to watch the San Francisco Giants. Wind whipped through the stands as the fog rolled over the stadium walls. When we experience that same hot chocolate flavor years later, those memories come flooding back; memories my family and I share. At Guittard, it's our job to create consistent flavors in our chocolate and enable those memories, which this book celebrates.

In its most basic form, food binds us together. With chocolate, we celebrate life and culture—whether it's connecting you to the farmer who cultivated the cacao beans or the family that made the chocolate or the moment around the table when you can relish the joy of sharing the chocolate.

**Sharing Our Time-Tested Family Recipes**
Just as Guittard Chocolate Company has evolved over generations, so has our collection of recipes. This book brings together the best of the best of our family favorites. The pages are filled with easy-to-follow, classic recipes in which chocolate is the hero. We made some adjustments here and there to update the recipes for today's baker. Through carefully selected ingredients, each recipe brings out and celebrates the flavor of a beautifully crafted chocolate.

One chapter of recipes is written by Guittard chef, teacher, and trainer Donald Wressell. These recipes bring in a pastry chef's sensibilities, and are slightly more challenging than the other recipes in the book but are well worth the effort.

Beyond my family's long history, chocolate carries its own story, which began long before cacao beans came to our factory. When I eat chocolate, the stories that fill my mind are of the families who've made cacao their livelihood for centuries, the history behind some of our oldest formulas, and the first time I had a chocolate chip cookie. I love a recipe that lets the true, full flavor of good chocolate shine. With that flavor, you can taste the culture and history behind the chocolate.

I have a soft spot for anything sweet, especially if chocolate is included. And a lazy Sunday afternoon will inevitably turn into my own personal bake-off that leaves me driving around the city finding homes for my fresh-out-of-the oven goodies. I make some staple items without a recipe and then I have a whole "to-try" list that keeps me on my toes. One of my favorite things to do is work our chocolate into recipes that sound promising. Tasting the freshly roasted beans in-house, the refined product, the final tempered hand-crafted bar, and then using that product in a sweet I bake in my studio-apartment kitchen is a process that brings new meaning to the idea of homemade.

My granny's Chocolate Persimmon Cake (page 36) was a longstanding favorite in the family. The cake took a multi-decade-long hiatus, until my uncle Hoddy and cousin Jennifer decided to revive the tradition. There was only one problem—no one had the complete recipe written down. All we had was a puzzle with missing ingredients and steps. Between the two of them, they put together a working recipe, and the cake now appears on the family dessert table every Christmas Eve, bringing back childhood memories for some and making new ones for those in my generation. When you take the first bite of this cake, you'll become totally immersed in the flavors—the rich depth of the chocolate and the way it makes persimmon something new and delicious.

Few foods evoke the same kind of passionate response that chocolate does. This book is written by a chocolate lover, and the recipes come from generations of chocolate lovers. I hope these pages will inspire you to see chocolate from a fresh perspective and to taste it with a new appreciation.

**A Legacy of Enjoying Fine Chocolate, from Our Family to Yours**

This book is about chocolate, but it's also about family. It's about the Guittard family and our extended family. It's about how chocolate traditions come to be part of your family's story, too, through making, sharing, and eating together. It's about bringing people together around a food that evokes strong and happy memories.

Our goal for this book is to help you feel comfortable cooking with chocolate while also connecting you to its history, culture, and artistry. All of us at Guittard hope that making and savoring these treats become a part of your family's history just as they are a part of ours.

Welcome to the family—welcome to Guittard.

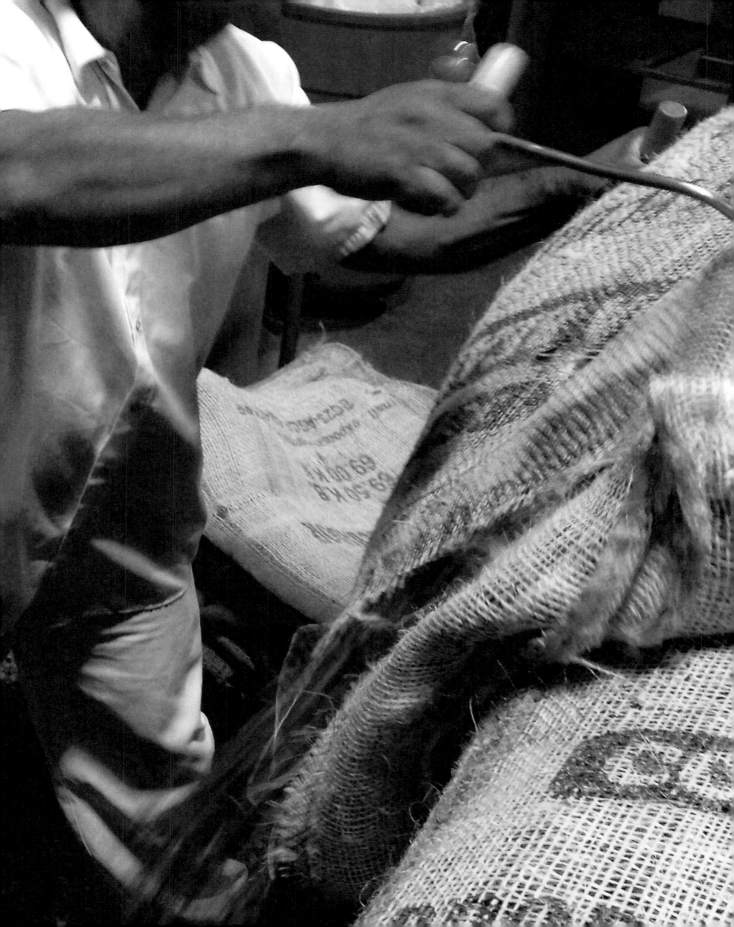

# Making Guittard Chocolate, from Bean to Bar

During the five generations of Guittard chocolate-making, we've learned a thing or two about cacao beans. The finest chocolate begins with cacao beans that we source from around the world for their quality and their sustainability. We select single-origin beans (beans from one geographic region) for their exclusive flavors and attributes, and then customize blends and formulas to deliver a distinctive chocolate experience.

Cacao is grown +/- 20 degrees latitude from the equator, where there is sufficient rainfall and rich soil to nurture the tree. The tree produces a fruit called a pod. The pod contains approximately forty beans (actually seeds, but we call them beans) surrounded by a delicious, slightly fruity and slightly sweet pulp.

Cacao is unique in that 95 percent of the world crop is produced on farms that are 10 acres [4 hectares] or less. Guittard uses superior shade-grown cacao, because the delicate pods need to be protected from direct sunlight during development for the beans to have the best flavor. And growing cacao under taller trees preserves the natural forest environment, which benefits native animals, plants, and the people who live nearby.

Cacao beans are harvested primarily from October through March, depending on the country, and pods can appear year-round. Although more labor intensive, frequent harvesting ensures that each cacao pod is perfectly ripe when picked. The pods are ripe in a window that's one-and-a-half to two weeks long. To harvest the pods, growers cut them off the tree, break them open, and remove the beans.

The farmers then ferment the beans until the flavors are perfect. Specific fermentation methods are one component to flavor development; fermentation, like farming, relies on experience. Each origin has its own traditions for bringing out the best of the cacao from their specific trees and *terroir* (the climate, and the geological and geographical influences on flavor). Beans are fermented in either wooden boxes, baskets, or piles on a drying bed, covered in banana leaves. Farmers ferment their beans anywhere from three to seven days, depending on the specific bean type. It's not easy to achieve the perfect flavor pitch for each bean. The key challenge is getting the beans to a particular temperature.

After the fermentation process, growers spread out the beans on the ground or on drying beds to dry naturally in the sun, sometimes using a rake to create traditional patterns as they turn the beans for even drying. Because sun-drying enhances natural chocolate flavor and avoids the pitfalls of other drying methods, Guittard chocolate is made almost exclusively from sun-dried beans.

Small batches of these cacao beans are sent from the farm to our factory for evaluation. Guittard accepts only the highest-quality beans to make into chocolate; each bean must deliver as much flavor as possible. Once the cacao beans are selected, they're roasted. Then, they go through a process called winnowing to remove the shell. The nibs (the inside of the bean, minus the shell) are then slowly ground on stone mills until the particles are broken down to release the cacao butter and let the flavor bouquet blossom. The substance becomes a rich, dark, fantastically aromatic but bitter liquid, called *chocolate liquor* or *cacao mass*. At this point, other ingredients may be added, such as sugar, additional cacao butter, and milk (for milk chocolate). The mixture is then refined further, taking it from a thick paste and turning it into a delicate flake that, upon touching your tongue, melts with a burst of chocolate flavor.

Conching is the crucial next step in flavor development. Conching is a step in which the delicate flake from the refiner is worked against itself with large paddles, gradually turning it from a powder to a slightly sticky paste-like mass to a progressively thinner liquid, arriving at a smooth, rich, refined, and luscious final product. Conching times, temperatures, and mixing profiles determine the nuances and complexities that appear in the chocolate's flavor.

The final step in chocolate-making is tempering. Tempering is an art in itself, in which the entire focus is to establish crystals in a portion of the cacao butter that will give the finished chocolate a shiny look, a perfect snap, and a decadent melt. Achieving a proper temper requires knowing the specific characteristics of the chocolate in order to calculate the exact temperature and time that it must be held at that temperature for the crystalization to occur, and for the chocolate to then be cooled at precisely the right temperature. The tempered chocolate is then molded into bars, wafers, or chips, or, in the case of the confectioner, used in delicious bonbons.

# Chocolate-Making Terms

Knowing the terms used in chocolate-making is the first step to understanding the craftsmanship that goes into each bar, chip, wafer, and powder. And it will help you select just the right chocolate for your baking and confectionery adventures.

## % CACAO

The percentage number, often seen on the chocolate product's label and written like this: "72% cacao," tells you the proportion of the chocolate derived from the cacao bean—including the cacao mass (also called chocolate liquor) plus any added cacao butter. For instance, a 72% cacao chocolate might be made up of 72 percent cacao mass plus 28 percent sugar and other ingredients *or* it might be made up of 65 percent cacao mass with 7 percent added cacao butter with 28 percent sugar and other ingredients.

## CACAO BUTTER

Cacao butter is the pure fat that naturally occurs in cacao beans. A process of pressing chocolate liquor separates the cacao butter from the cacao solids. The cacao butter carries with it a delicate but rich aroma of the beans from which it was derived. The cacao solids are then reground into the fine particles that we call cocoa powder. Cacao butter is not a dairy product. It is called a butter because it melts just below the temperature of our palates, giving chocolate that crisp, silky melt-in-the-mouth feel. "Prime pressed cacao butter" is the cacao butter from specially selected flavor cacao beans.

**Added Cacao Butter:** At Guittard, we add cacao butter to arrive at a certain viscosity. It makes the final chocolate smoother, and the press butter we use further enhances the flavor of the chocolate. When cacao butter is added to the chocolate recipe, it is included as part of the percent cacao because it is derived from the cacao bean as is the chocolate liquor.

## CACAO NIBS

When a cacao bean is roasted and then winnowed (which means it's cleaned and the outer shell is blown away), what's left behind is the cocoa nib: a crunchy, intensely flavorful bite of unsweetened, unprocessed heart of the cacao bean that will later become chocolate. To make chocolate, we then begin grinding this nib, but on its own, it's a great substitute for nuts in a salad or in a cookie.

## CACAO MASS (CHOCOLATE LIQUOR)

The cacao mass is the substance produced when the ground nibs are further ground into finer and finer particles before any other ingredients are added, including cacao butter. It is a rich, absolutely intense liquid that is very bitter. It is liquid at warm temperatures and solid at room temperature. Most chocolate liquor contains 50 to 58 percent cacao butter and 42 to 50 percent cacao solids (cocoa powder).

## CHOCOLATE

In the United States, chocolate is governed by "standards of identity" under the jurisdiction of the Food and Drug Administration (FDA). Per these standards, chocolate is not allowed to contain any fat other than pure cacao butter or dairy butter oil. Vegetable fats are not permitted. The standards also describe the required composition of various forms of chocolate. Whether we call it bitter or semisweet is left to the manufacturer. The standards of composition are as follows.

**Unsweetened chocolate:** Must contain 50 to 60 percent cacao butter (and 40 to 50 percent cacao solids) and no sugar.

**Bittersweet chocolate (or semisweet chocolate):** Must be at least 35 percent chocolate liquor. On the grocery shelf, you'll often see both bittersweet and semisweet chocolate. While a single standard of identity is the same for both products, manufacturers make a distinction that is somewhat arbitrary but helpful when specifying for recipes. Bittersweet chocolate is often defined as 65 to 99% cacao; semisweet is typically 35 to 65% cacao.

**Milk chocolate:** Must contain at least 10 percent chocolate liquor and 12 percent milk solids in addition to sugar and cacao butter.

**White chocolate:** Must contain at least 20 percent pure cacao butter and a minimum of 14 percent milk solids. The balance is sugar and other ingredients. White chocolate contains cacao butter from the cacao beans as the main component, along with milk, sugar, and other ingredients. It does not contain any of the chocolate liquor that is used to make milk chocolate or dark chocolate. The flavor and delicate bouquet of white chocolate is heavenly and is influenced by the flavor and bouquet of the cacao butter used. At Guittard, we use prime pressed cacao butter.

## CHOCOLATE BLOOM

Chocolate bloom is a white, powdery haze that forms on the surface of chocolate; it can also appear as a tan, grainy or crumbly structure throughout the chocolate bar. It's caused by the cacao butter having partially melted and then resolidified because of fluctuations in temperature. Bloomed chocolate may be unattractive and might not taste as good but it is safe to eat. You can restore the chocolate's dark, glossy finish and characteristic snap by melting and then retempering it.

## COCOA POWDER (*SEE ALSO* DUTCH-PROCESSED COCOA POWDER)

Cocoa powder is made from the solids that remain after cacao butter is extracted or pressed from chocolate liquor. Cocoa powder is categorized by the amount of cacao butter that remains after pressing. Retail cocoa products can range from 10 to 24 percent fat.

## COUVERTURE

French for "coating," couverture chocolate contains at least 32 percent cacao butter, which is perfect for covering (or enrobing) chocolate pieces. The term is defined for legal purposes only in France, although this French definition has become an accepted standard worldwide.

## DUTCH-PROCESSED COCOA POWDER

*Dutching* is a term used to describe cocoa powder that is treated with an alkalizing agent to modify the acidity and darken the color. When you "Dutch" cocoa powder, you get a milder chocolate flavor. Chefs use Dutch-processed cocoa powder to deliver dimension and balance and often use the dark color to achieve a more intense, richer color in their finished products.

## TEMPERING

Tempering is the process of turning melted chocolate into a solid mass of stable cacao butter crystals with a fine, even-grained texture and a glossy finish. Tempering is done by warming chocolate, mixing it to a perfect consistency, and then cooling it with carefully controlled mixing and hold times from 85 to 88°F [29 to 31°C] for milk chocolate or 88 to 90°F [31 to 32°C] for dark chocolate.

These days, you'll see a range of dark chocolate as well as bittersweet chocolate, milk chocolate, natural cocoa powder, Dutch-processed cocoa powder, and even cacao nibs on your grocery store shelves. But how do you use each of these forms of chocolate? There are no hard-and-fast rules. I've found it enlightening (and fun) to make dessert recipes twice, once from a bittersweet chocolate and once from a semisweet chocolate, to discover my own preferences.

The recipes in this book suggest an appropriate kind of chocolate to use for each. However, with most of the recipes in this book, you can use your favorite kind of chocolate if you don't have the variety of chocolate called for or if you prefer a different flavor. Feel free to experiment with different cacao percentages. If you're like me and love really dark chocolate, substitute bittersweet for semisweet, for instance. If you like something a little lighter, try milk chocolate instead of semisweet.

## BAKING CHOCOLATE: CHIPS, BARS, AND WAFERS

Guittard uses three different formats for baking chocolate: chips, bars, and wafers. Chocolate chips have less cacao butter, which is what keeps them upright. Chips work exceptionally well in a cookie because they provide structure and help hold up the cookie, but they aren't ideal for melting. Chocolate wafers and chocolate baking bars have more cacao butter, which makes them ideal for melting.

Baking bars are easy to break apart and weigh and measure in ounces and grams, while wafers are easy to use and perfect for measuring in cups. Bars and wafers are excellent substitutes for each other if you can find only one at your local grocery store. Just because they are labeled "baking bars" doesn't mean you can't eat them. I do it all the time.

The following forms of Guittard baking chocolate come in different levels of darkness, containing more or less sugar and different cacao mass percentages.

**Guittard Unsweetened Chocolate Baking Bars (100% cacao):** This baking bar is a distinct liquor that delivers flavors of fruit and spices amid a deep base chocolate. Bitterness gives way to a subtle floral sweetness, adding a unique layer of complexity.

## DARK CHOCOLATE

One step below unsweetened chocolate, dark chocolate gives you a highly intense chocolate flavor.

**Guittard Nocturne Extra Dark Chocolate Bar (91% cacao):** This extra dark, multibean blend is uniquely complex, with a layered approach of red fruit and nut notes held up with a solid chocolate base.

**Guittard Extra Dark Chocolate Baking Chips (63% cacao):** Extra dark, extra intense, with subtle notes of vanilla.

## BITTERSWEET CHOCOLATE

Bittersweet chocolate has an intense flavor with some sweetness (unlike a 99% cacao, which is not sweet at all). I like to use this in soufflés, puddings, cakes, and chocolate drinks. You can buy it in bars, chips, or wafers.

**Guittard Organic Bittersweet Chocolate Baking Wafers (74% cacao):** A bold chocolate with spice and dried fruit notes with balanced sour and tannin undertones.

**Guittard Bittersweet Chocolate Baking Bars (70% cacao):** Chocolate flavors linger throughout with bright red fruit and cherry notes. A tart aftertaste lends an astringency that helps carry the peak endnotes of this bittersweet chocolate into a deep chocolate finish.

## SEMISWEET CHOCOLATE

Semisweet chocolate is sort of a standard, with a cacao percentage found in most baking chips that you use for cookies, brownies, cakes, and candies. You can also buy this chocolate in bars, chips, or wafers.

**Guittard Organic Semisweet Chocolate Baking Wafers (66% cacao):** A base of deep chocolate gives way to fresh berries and spice with lingering floral accents of jasmine.

**Guittard Semisweet Chocolate Baking Bars (64% cacao):** These baking bars deliver a complex chocolate with peaks of tart fruit and cherry top notes. Floral aromatics lead to an astringent lingering sensation with chocolatey endnotes.

**Guittard Akoma Extra Semisweet Chocolate Chips (55% cacao):** The name *Akoma* represents "heart" in the traditional Adinkra symbols of West Africa, where cacao beans for this Fair Trade chocolate are grown. With a slightly higher percentage than our traditional semisweet chips, Akoma delivers a deep chocolate flavor.

**Guittard Super Cookie Chips (48% cacao):** There's deep chocolate flavor in this semisweet chip with a unique shape.

**Guittard Semisweet Chocolate Baking Chips (46% cacao):** Our classic semisweet chip delivers hints of vanilla in a smooth chocolate base.

## MILK CHOCOLATE

Just as the name suggests, milk chocolate contains milk. It also contains more sugar than the other forms of chocolate. You can use milk chocolate in place of a darker chocolate when you want a sweeter, less intense flavor. You can buy it in chips or wafers.

**Guittard Organic Milk Chocolate Baking Wafers (38% cacao):** This organic milk chocolate delivers a milky-dark chocolate taste. Fruity and malty tones add unique complexity.

**Guittard Milk Chocolate Baking Chips (31% cacao):** The first milk chocolate baking chip of its kind, this extra-large chip delivers smooth, creamy dairy notes with a classic chocolate flavor.

## WHITE CHOCOLATE

You often hear people say that white chocolate isn't real chocolate. This is partly true because it doesn't have any cacao solids—that's why it's white. If, however, it contains 20 percent or more cacao butter, it can be called white chocolate. You can buy white chocolate in chips or purchase larger packs available to pastry chefs at select online retailers.

**Guittard Choc-Au-Lait Baking Chips:** A creamy and milky white chocolate with the essence of real vanilla.

## OTHER TYPES OF BAKING CHIPS

These baking chips are similar in consistency to chocolate chips but each adds a distinct flavor.

**Guittard Butterscotch Baking Chips:** A rich butterscotch flavor with the essence of real vanilla that pairs deliciously with dark and milk chocolate.

**Guittard Green Mint Baking Chips:** A smooth, cool mint flavor (and color), perfect for adding to brownies, cookies, and cakes.

## SINGLE-ORIGIN BARS

*Single-origin chocolate* means that the beans were grown in one place. If you think of chocolate as similar to wine, using beans from one place is like making wine with grapes from one vineyard or region. The benefit of single-origin chocolate is that you can taste very specific flavors—perhaps red berries, citrus, or nuts—that may not be as evident when beans from different regions are blended together.

Single-origin chocolate bars are a great way to experience the inherent flavor profiles of cacao beans from different regions. The subtle flavors of the varietals, *terroir*, and post-harvest techniques come across when you taste single-origin chocolates side by side. You can break bars into small pieces, and taste, smell, and breathe in the various subtleties. This may be the best way to find which flavors in chocolate (and which chocolate-growing regions) most appeal to you.

You can also use single-origin chocolates as flavor notes in recipes, or even to highlight flavors or ingredients you're using. The inherently tart Madagascar chocolate might be used if you're looking to punch up a quick bread that has some lemon in it; toss in a Colombian single-origin if you want to emphasize the spices in a cookie recipe. Play around with single-origin chocolates in your favorite recipes to see how they change the end flavors. You'll be surprised what a little single-origin can do.

**Guittard Ambanja Bittersweet Bar, Madagascar (65% cacao):** Rarified Criollo cacao beans from Madagascar are carefully handcrafted into this delicious chocolate. It mingles tart and fruity essences with one-of-a-kind, deep, rich chocolate flavor.

**Guittard Chucuri Bittersweet Bar, Colombia (65% cacao):** Deep, lingering chocolate flavors are accented by hints of spice.

**Guittard Quevedo Bittersweet Bar, Ecuador (65% cacao):** Extremely dark color foreshadows its powerful but flowery chocolate taste. The intensity of this rarified Forestero varietal produces rich green tea and slight nut flavors with a lingering banana and pound cake finish.

**Guittard Sur del Lago Bittersweet Bar, Venezuela (65% cacao):** Complex chocolate flavors underlie subtle hints of red berry fruit.

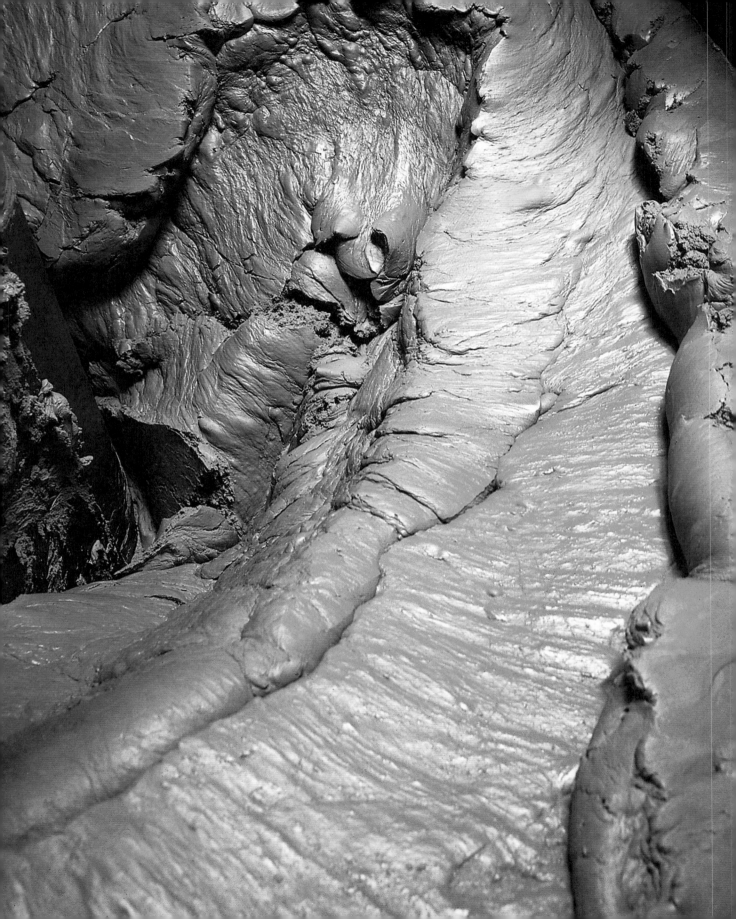

## COCOA POWDER

Cocoa powder was first documented in the early nineteenth century in Amsterdam. Pressing most of the cacao butter out of the beans left a powder that could keep for a very long time. The cacao beans at that time were often much harsher than the beans we source today. The Dutch softened those harsh acidic flavors by adding alkali, which also gave the cocoa powder a very dark color—what we see when we think of a true devil's food cake.

**Guittard Cocoa Rouge Unsweetened Cocoa Powder:** The intense bittersweet character; rich, deep red color; robust, fudge-like flavor; and full chocolate essence is ideal in baked goods such as cakes and pastries. The unique yet subtle Dutched flavor, which is both intense and mellow, provides a perfect complement to other ingredients.

**Guittard Grand Cacao Drinking Chocolate, Sweet Ground Cocoa:** Premium chocolate is finely ground and added into high-quality, old-fashioned, Dutch-processed unsweetened cocoa powder to achieve intense chocolate flavor; a full-bodied, creamy texture; rich, red-brown, dark chocolate color; and comforting, homemade, pudding-like, baked chocolate aromas.

## DAIRY

**Butter:** Unless specified, use a high-quality unsalted butter. This allows you to control the salt in each recipe, because the amount of salt in different salted butters can vary widely.

**Heavy Whipping Cream:** Heavy whipping cream (also called heavy cream) has a high fat content (between 36 and 40 percent) and doubles in size when whipped. If you add a little sugar, you get whipped cream (see page 170). It is also used in smaller doses for a smooth chocolate ganache (see page 165) and in chocolate bread pudding (see page 42).

**Milk and Yogurt:** Our recipes call for whole milk, buttermilk, and full-fat yogurt instead of low-fat or non-fat because a higher fat content means a more tender, moist baked good. You will notice a drier crumb in breads and muffins if you use a lower-fat milk or yogurt.

## EGGS

Eggs play an important role in baking. They provide structure and leavening. They work with the flour to determine height and density of the finished good. Use the freshest eggs you can find.

## FLOUR

While most bakers are familiar with all-purpose flour, there are many different types of flours to choose from. For most recipes, all-purpose flour is your best bet, since it's versatile enough for many applications. Some of our recipes are old but we've updated them by incorporating different types of flours for half of the all-purpose flour the recipe calls for. Using a variety of flours

is a quick and easy way to get a slightly different taste and texture or to add a healthful twist to a classic recipe. The recipes in this book call for whole-wheat and light rye flours, but feel free to experiment with other varieties. Whole-wheat flour adds nuttiness to baked goods, is more healthful, and has more fiber than all-purpose flour. You'll find both white (unbleached) whole-wheat flour and whole-wheat flour at your grocery store. Whole-wheat flour has a darker color and is nuttier, while white whole-wheat flour is made from white wheat berries instead of red wheat berries, so the flavor is mild in comparison, and it's lighter in color. Rye flour contains more nutrients than refined wheat flour, makes a denser baked good, and gives a deeper, more complex flavor. Rye flour can be light or dark, but I call for light because dark rye flour is a bit too sour for these recipes.

You'll be able to see a slight difference in color if you substitute a darker flour for all-purpose flour. For this reason, I usually call for whole-wheat or rye flour in recipes that use cocoa powder or melted chocolate instead of recipes that are light in color, such as chocolate chip cookies, so as not to show the color difference of the flour.

## SALT

Whenever possible, avoid using table salt for baking because it often has a slight metallic flavor from the added iodine. Kosher or sea salt are preferred since they are purer forms of salt.

Some of the recipes call for fleur de sel, which is a high-quality sea salt. The flakes are larger than traditional sea salt, which makes for a better crunch. If you don't have fleur de sel, substitute traditional sea salt.

## SUGAR

The recipes call for seven different types of sugar: granulated, superfine, raw or turbinado, Demerara, confectioners', light brown sugar, and dark brown sugar. Granulated sugar is the basic white sugar that you probably have in your kitchen. Superfine sugar, also known as baker's sugar or castor sugar, has small crystals that dissolve quickly. Raw or turbinado sugar has been minimally processed compared to white sugar, so it is made up of large, brown, crunchy crystals. The brown color indicates that there is molasses in it (the molasses has been extracted from white sugars), which gives it a deeper, more complex flavor than white sugar. Demerara sugar is also less refined than white sugar; it has a little more crunch and bigger grains than turbinado. Confectioners' sugar, or powdered sugar, is a very fine, powdery sugar with a small amount of anti-caking agent in it, which makes it perfect for frostings. Light and dark brown sugar are more processed than raw sugar but less processed than granulated sugar. Brown sugar is moist and has a soft texture with varying amounts of molasses depending on whether it's light or dark (about 3.5 percent for light and 6.5 percent for dark).

## VANILLA

These recipes usually call for vanilla extract. I always use organic high-quality pure vanilla extract. But a few recipes call for a vanilla bean. (See Note: Using Vanilla Beans, page 114.) Vanilla beans offer a more intense vanilla flavor, but if you don't have a vanilla bean, you can substitute 1 tsp vanilla extract for 1 vanilla bean.

# G

# GUITTARD & CO'S.

## GRAPE sugar TARTAR

GUITTARD & CO'S.
CHOCOLATE

# BAKING

## *Chapter 1*
# BREAKFAST

---

# MORNING GLORY SCONES

Hot chocolate was a constant in our house when I was growing up. Sometimes we mixed our cocoa powder with milk, and other times we whisked hot milk into melted chocolate. Both were equally delicious but made for decidedly different drinking experiences. This scone recipe uses our hot chocolate mix, which is made of both cocoa powder and chocolate flakes, contributing a distinct fudgy texture. The dried cranberries and sugar topping add extra sweetness to every bite. I go all out on chocolate and serve these with mugs of hot chocolate.

1⅔ cups [200 g] all-purpose flour

⅔ cup [70 g] Guittard Grand Cacao Drinking Chocolate (sweet ground cocoa)

2 tsp baking powder

5 Tbsp [70 g] unsalted butter

¾ cup [125 g] dried cranberries (optional)

⅔ cup [160 ml] whole milk, plus 1 tsp

1 Tbsp raw or turbinado sugar

Preheat the oven to 425°F [220°C]. Line a baking sheet with parchment paper.

Using a food processor, pulse the flour, hot chocolate mix, and baking powder for about 15 seconds to combine. Cut the butter into five slices, add to the flour mixture, and pulse just until incorporated. Add the cranberries (if using) and ⅔ cup [160 ml] milk and pulse until the ingredients come together in a ball.

Lightly flour your hands and transfer the dough to a lightly floured work surface. Form the dough into a 9-in [23-cm] circle about 1 in [2.5 cm] thick. Brush the top with the remaining 1 tsp milk and sprinkle evenly with the raw sugar. Cut the dough into eight wedges and place the wedges on the prepared baking sheet, leaving 1 in [2.5 cm] between each wedge.

Bake for 12 to 15 minutes, until the scones are puffed and cracked on top. Using a spatula, immediately move the scones to a wire rack to cool. Store in an airtight container at room temperature for up to 4 days; or tightly wrapped in plastic wrap in the freezer for up to 2 months. To defrost, move the wrapped scones to the refrigerator overnight. Reheat in a 375°F [190°C] oven for 3 to 5 minutes.

**MAKES 8 SCONES**

# CHOCOLATE CHERRY SCONES

These fruit-and-chocolate scones make a regular appearance at my potluck brunches. Three kinds of chocolate—semisweet chocolate, white chocolate, and cocoa powder—ensure a serious chocolate flavor that's balanced by the tart bite of dried cherries. These scones can also be served for dessert with a dollop of Whipped Cream (page 170) or crème fraîche. For light, fluffy scones, start with very cold butter and don't overmix the dough.

3 oz [85 g] Guittard Semisweet Chocolate Baking Bars, broken into pieces

½ cup [85 g] Guittard Choc-Au-Lait Baking Chips (white chocolate)

½ cup [50 g] Guittard Cocoa Rouge (Dutch-processed unsweetened cocoa powder)

½ cup [85 g] dried cherries

½ cup [100 g] sugar

2½ cups [300 g] all-purpose flour

2 tsp baking powder

1 tsp baking soda

½ tsp salt

6 Tbsp [85 g] unsalted butter, chilled

1 large egg

¾ cup [180 ml] full-fat buttermilk

CONTINUED

Preheat the oven to 400°F [200°C]. Line two baking sheets with parchment paper.

Using a food processor, pulse the semisweet chocolate, white chocolate, cocoa powder, cherries, and sugar until the chocolate is finely ground, about 30 seconds.

In a large bowl, combine the flour, baking powder, baking soda, and salt. Add the chocolate mixture to the flour mixture and use your hands to mix well. Cut the cold butter into ½-in [12-mm] cubes and add to the mixture. Using a pastry cutter or two knives, cut the butter into the mixture until the mixture resembles wet sand.

In a liquid measuring cup, lightly beat the egg with the buttermilk. Pour the buttermilk mixture into the dry ingredients and blend with a hand mixer until combined.

Lightly flour your hands and transfer the dough to a lightly floured work surface. Form the dough into a mound and divide it into three equal portions. Flatten each piece of dough into a 5-in [12-cm] circle about 1 in [2.5 cm] thick. Cut one circle into quarters to form four wedges. Place the wedges on the prepared baking sheet so there is 1½ in [4 cm] between them. Repeat with the two remaining circles of dough.

Bake for 15 minutes, or until the scones are puffed and cracked on top. Using a spatula, immediately move the scones to a wire rack to cool. Store in an airtight container at room temperature for up to 4 days; or wrapped tightly in plastic wrap in the freezer for up to 2 months. To defrost, move the wrapped scones to the refrigerator overnight. Reheat in a 375°F [190°C] oven for 3 to 5 minutes.

**MAKES 12 SCONES**

# MORNING MUFFINS

These breakfast muffins are chock-full of good-for-you morning staples: oats, cinnamon, and applesauce. I love that the rich bottom note of semisweet chocolate in this recipe makes all these healthful elements even more satisfying. When I start my day at 5 A.M., one of these muffins keeps me going until my 10:30 chocolate break. These muffins are perfect right out of the oven for a Sunday brunch, but they can also be made ahead, frozen, and warmed up or toasted just before you run out the door.

½ cup [60 g] all-purpose flour

¼ cup [30 g] light rye flour

1 tsp baking soda

½ tsp ground cinnamon

⅛ tsp salt

¾ cup [210 g] unsweetened applesauce

¼ cup [60 ml] whole milk

¼ cup [60 ml] vegetable oil

¼ cup [80 g] honey

1 tsp freshly grated orange zest

¾ cup [60 g] old-fashioned rolled oats

1 cup [170 g] Guittard Semisweet Chocolate Baking Chips

Preheat the oven to 400°F [200°C]. Lightly butter the cups of a standard 12-cup muffin tin.

In a small bowl, combine the all-purpose flour, rye flour, baking soda, cinnamon, and salt. Set aside.

In a large bowl, with a hand mixer, beat together the applesauce, milk, vegetable oil, honey, and orange zest until smooth, about 2 minutes. Stir in the flour mixture until just combined. Fold in the oats and chocolate chips. Spoon the batter into the prepared muffin cups, filling them three-quarters full.

Bake for 13 to 15 minutes, until a toothpick inserted into the center of a muffin comes out clean. Let the muffins cool in the pan for 5 minutes, then remove to a wire rack to cool completely. Store, wrapped tightly in plastic wrap in the freezer, for up to 1 month. To defrost, microwave for 1 minute on the defrost setting, then lightly toast in a toaster oven before serving.

**MAKES 12 MUFFINS**

# CHOCOLATE PERSIMMON CAKE

This persimmon cake recipe might be the oldest recipe in the book. It was created in the 1890s by someone on my paternal grandmother's side of the family. It's a gem of a recipe that can add a little excitement to a brunch spread or star on the dessert table when baked in a Bundt pan. Even people who aren't familiar with persimmons love this cake. For one reason or another, the cake vanished from the Christmas Eve table for years until recently, when my uncle Hoddy and cousin Jennifer took it upon themselves to bring it back—not an easy task, given that my granny never wrote down the complete recipe. They worked in the kitchen until they were able to duplicate the cake, and now once again it takes pride of place at the holiday table. The recipe includes both cocoa powder and bitter-sweet chocolate for a silky fudgelike texture. To get the freshest persimmon pulp, choose fresh, ripe Hachiya persimmons that are extra soft. While the traditional method calls for steaming this cake, we've simplified the recipe so it can be baked in the oven. If persimmons are out of season, substitute 1½ cups [365 g] pumpkin purée.

½ cup [60 g] all-purpose flour

½ cup [60 g] whole-wheat flour

6 Tbsp [30 g] Guittard Cocoa Rouge (Dutch-processed unsweetened cocoa powder)

2 tsp baking soda

½ tsp salt

1 tsp ground cinnamon

½ tsp ground cloves

½ cup [110 g] unsalted butter, at room temperature

½ cup [100 g] granulated sugar

½ cup [100 g] firmly packed light brown sugar

2 large eggs

½ cup [120 ml] full-fat plain yogurt

1½ cups [400 g] persimmon pulp

½ cup [170 g] Guittard Extra Dark Chocolate Baking Chips

Preheat the oven to 375°F [190°C]. Lightly butter a 6-cup [1.4-L] Bundt pan or cut a 9-in [23-cm] piece of parchment paper, lightly butter the parchment, then lay the parchment paper, butter-side up, inside a 9-by-5-by-3-in [23-by-12-by-7.5-cm] loaf pan, leaving the extra parchment sticking out the sides; the parchment will not cover the two 5-in [12-cm] ends.

In a medium bowl, combine the all-purpose flour, whole-wheat flour, cocoa powder, baking soda, salt, cinnamon, and cloves. Set aside.

In a large bowl, with a hand mixer, beat together the butter, granulated sugar, and brown sugar until light and smooth, about 3 minutes. Add the eggs, one at a time, and the yogurt and mix after each addition until smooth. Add the persimmon pulp and the flour mixture, alternating between the two, in four additions, mixing after

CONTINUED

each addition until well combined. Fold in the chocolate chips. Pour the batter into the prepared pan.

Bake for 1 hour, or until a toothpick inserted into the center comes out clean. Let the cake sit on a wire rack for 10 minutes to cool. Invert a second wire rack over the top of the cake. Using both hands, flip the cake and rack so the pan is upside down on the rack. Gently shake the pan to release the cake onto the rack. Flip the cake back over so it is right-side up. Allow to cool completely, 2 to 4 hours, then wrap tightly in plastic wrap. This is best served the morning after you make it. Store wrapped tightly in plastic wrap at room temperature for up to 5 days; or in the freezer for up to 2 months. To defrost, move the wrapped cake to the refrigerator overnight. Reheat in a 350°F [180°C] oven for 5 to 10 minutes or until heated through.

**MAKES ONE 6-CUP [1.4-L] BUNDT CAKE OR ONE 9-BY-5-IN [23-BY-12-CM] LOAF**

**Variation for Granny's Pudding:** To make this cake the way my granny did, pour the prepared batter into a pudding pan. Set up a hot water bath (see Note: Melting Chocolate, page 51) and set the pudding pan over the simmering water, cover with a large saucepan lid, and steam for 2 hours. Let cool for 10 minutes and proceed as directed.

# CHOCOLATE COCONUT BREAD

I love a good quick bread, and this is one of my favorites. A few slices make a perfect breakfast or snack with tea. The raw sugar topping adds an unexpected crunch and the addition of coconut lends a choice texture that instantly transports me to the islands of Hawaii. Any high-quality bittersweet chocolate will do here, but using a single-origin chocolate can impart a unique flavor profile that adds dimension to the bread. I prefer our Chucuri Colombian chocolate because it brings spicy notes that complement the coconut. Sometimes I make this recipe into a dessert by doubling the amount of chocolate, working from the premise that you can't get too much of a good thing. This bread is best when served the day after you make it.

1½ cups [180 g] all-purpose flour

1½ tsp baking powder

½ tsp salt

1 cup [90 g] unsweetened shredded coconut

½ cup [110 g] unsalted butter, melted and cooled

½ cup [100 g] granulated sugar

1 large egg, lightly beaten

¼ cup [60 ml] whole milk

¼ cup [60 ml] coconut water

½ tsp vanilla extract

3 oz [75 g] Guittard Chucuri Bittersweet Chocolate, broken into small pieces

1 Tbsp raw or turbinado sugar

Preheat the oven to 350°F [180°C]. Butter and flour a 9-by-5-by-3-in [23-by-12-by-7.5-cm] loaf pan.

In a medium bowl, combine the flour, baking powder, and salt. Stir in the shredded coconut. Set aside.

In a large bowl, with a hand mixer, blend together the butter, granulated sugar, egg, milk, coconut water, and vanilla until well combined. Add the flour mixture and mix until just combined. Fold in the chocolate. Pour the batter into the prepared loaf pan. Sprinkle the raw sugar over the batter.

Bake for 55 minutes, or until a toothpick inserted into the center comes out clean. Let the bread cool in the pan for 15 minutes. Loosen the bread from the pan by running a knife around the sides. Invert a wire rack over the top of the bread. Using both hands, flip the bread and rack so the loaf pan is upside down on the rack. Gently shake the pan to release the bread onto the rack. Flip the bread back over so it is sugar-side up. Allow to cool completely, then wrap tightly in plastic wrap and let rest overnight. Store wrapped tightly in plastic wrap at room temperature for up to 5 days; or in the freezer for up to 2 months. To defrost, move the wrapped bread to the refrigerator overnight. Reheat in a 350°F [180°C] oven for 5 to 10 minutes or until heated through.

**MAKES ONE 9-BY-5-IN [23-BY-12-CM] LOAF**

# NOHO KAI CHOCOLATE BANANA BREAD

My Auntie Jill used to make this bread whenever she had visitors at her little house on the hill above Kapaa on Kauai. We would slice it up for an early-morning, presurfing breakfast or we'd snack on it when we came home from the beach, sand between our toes, salt still in our hair. If you like banana bread, this variation is sure to become one of your favorites, too. The key to great banana bread is waiting for your bananas to get really ripe and freckled. I use semisweet chocolate chips in this recipe, but bittersweet chocolate works well, too. While chocolate is the hero, for an extra dose of texture and sweetness, try folding in 1 cup [150 g] of halved ripe strawberries with the nuts and chocolate.

¾ cup [90 g] all-purpose flour

½ cup [60 g] whole-wheat flour

1 tsp baking soda

½ tsp salt

½ cup [110 g] unsalted butter, at room temperature

1 cup [200 g] sugar

3 ripe medium bananas, mashed

2 large eggs

½ cup [55 g] chopped walnuts, pecans, or macadamia nuts

1 cup [170 g] Guittard Semisweet Chocolate Baking Chips

Preheat the oven to 350°F [180°C]. Butter and flour a 9-by-5-by-3-in [23-by-12-by-7.5-cm] loaf pan.

In a small bowl, combine the all-purpose flour, whole-wheat flour, baking soda, and salt. Set aside.

In a large bowl, with a hand mixer, beat the butter and sugar until light and fluffy, about 3 minutes. Beat in the bananas and the eggs, one at a time, until well combined but still chunky. Gradually add the flour mixture and mix just until combined. Fold in the walnuts and chocolate chips. Pour the batter into the prepared loaf pan.

Bake for 55 to 65 minutes, or until a toothpick inserted into the center comes out clean. Let the bread cool in the pan for 15 minutes. Loosen the bread from the pan by running a knife around the sides. Invert a wire rack over the top of the pan. Using both hands, flip the bread and rack over so the loaf pan is upside down on the rack. Gently shake the pan to release the bread onto the rack. Flip the bread back over so it is right-side up. Allow to cool completely, then wrap tightly in plastic wrap. Store wrapped tightly in plastic wrap at room temperature for up to 5 days; or in the freezer for up to 2 months. To defrost, move the wrapped bread to the refrigerator overnight. Reheat in a 350°F [180°C] oven for 5 to 10 minutes or until heated through.

**MAKES ONE 9-BY-5-IN [23-BY-12-CM] LOAF**

# CHOCOLATE BREAD PUDDING

We've sponsored the California State Fair Chocolate Passion Contest for nearly fifteen years, and occasionally I get to hand out the medals. One year, the host asked me to share my favorite dessert. When I said bread pudding, there was an awkward silence followed by a few chuckles; apparently bread pudding wasn't a glamorous choice. I stand behind my answer and defy anyone to taste this luscious, rich, chocolate bread pudding and tell me it doesn't have a place in the pantheon of great desserts. For my bread pudding, I use challah—a fluffy, lightly sweet egg bread that's similar to brioche. If you like a really custardy pudding, reduce the amount of bread. Always use slightly stale bread when making a bread pudding, because it holds the custard better than a fresh loaf. "Tricks of the trade," as my mom likes to say.

**5 cups [400 g] cubed challah bread**

**½ cup [100 g] sugar**

**¼ cup [25 g] Guittard Cocoa Rouge (Dutch-processed unsweetened cocoa powder)**

**1½ tsp ground cinnamon**

**½ tsp ground cardamom**

**3 large eggs, plus 2 egg yolks**

**1 cup [240 ml] whole milk**

**1½ cups [360 ml] heavy whipping cream**

**1 tsp vanilla extract**

Put the bread cubes in an 8-by-11-in [20-by-28-cm] baking dish. Let the bread sit uncovered overnight (or use day-old bread).

Preheat the oven to 350°F [180°C].

In a small bowl, mix together the sugar, cocoa powder, cinnamon, and cardamom. Set aside.

In a large bowl, lightly beat the eggs and egg yolks, then whisk in the sugar mixture until combined. Add the milk, cream, and vanilla and whisk until combined. Pour the bread cubes into the mixture and carefully fold in with a rubber spatula. Then pour the milk-bread mixture back into the baking dish.

Bake for 40 to 45 minutes, or until the custard is set. Let the pudding cool completely before cutting it into squares and serving. Store covered with plastic wrap in the refrigerator for up to 2 days.

**MAKES ONE 8-BY-11-IN [20-BY-28-CM] PUDDING**

##### Chapter 2

# COOKIES

---

# CLASSIC CHOCOLATE CHIP COOKIES

Most of us grew up with this beloved cookie and you've seen recipes for chocolate chip cookies countless times on the backs of chocolate chip bags. But I promise you, this recipe, created in our test kitchens decades ago, really does produce the best classic chocolate chip cookie. We've improved the recipe over the years to make sure the butter-to-sugar-to-flour ratio yields a buttery, melt-in-your-mouth texture. A bit of vanilla gives way to epic amounts of chocolate chips with every bite. This cookie can be underbaked a touch if you're a fan of super-gooey goodness. When I'm feeling daring, I sprinkle a little fleur de sel on the tops right before putting them in the oven. Use high-quality unsalted butter and, of course, the best chocolate you can find. For me this means our tried-and-true semisweet chocolate chips. If you're ready to take this classic to the next level, try the variation for a giant chocolate chip cookie.

2½ cups [300 g] all-purpose flour

1 tsp baking soda

1 tsp salt

1 cup [220 g] unsalted butter, at room temperature

¾ cup [150 g] granulated sugar

¾ cup [150 g] firmly packed light brown sugar

2 large eggs

1 tsp vanilla extract

2 cups [340 g] Guittard Semisweet Chocolate Baking Chips

1 cup [110 g] chopped walnuts (optional)

Preheat the oven to 375°F [190°C]. Line two baking sheets with parchment paper.

In a medium bowl, combine the flour, baking soda, and salt. Set aside.

In a large bowl, with a hand mixer, beat together the butter, granulated sugar, and brown sugar until light and smooth, about 3 minutes. Beat in the eggs and vanilla until smooth. Gradually stir in the flour mixture until combined. Fold in the chocolate chips and the walnuts (if using). Drop the dough by rounded tablespoonsful onto the prepared baking sheets, leaving 2 in [5 cm] between the cookies; the cookies will spread as they bake.

Bake for 7 to 9 minutes, or until golden brown around the edges. Transfer the cookies to a wire rack to cool. Store in an airtight container at room temperature for up to 1 week.

**MAKES TWENTY-FOUR 3½-IN [9-CM] COOKIES**

**Variation for a giant chocolate chip cookie:**
Prepare the cookie dough as directed. Spread it evenly into a greased 9-in [23-cm] round cake pan. Bake at 375°F [190°C] for 20 to 25 minutes. Let cool completely in the pan, and cut into wedges. To serve, top with your favorite ice cream and Chocolate Shell (page 166).

**NOTE:** FREEZING COOKIE DOUGH. If you want freshly baked cookies any time, prepare the dough as directed and portion the cookies out on parchment paper as if you were going to bake them right away. You won't need much space between the cookies; just make sure they aren't touching. Place the cookies on the parchment paper–lined baking sheets in the freezer for 1 hour. Then, place all of the frozen cookie dough portions into a zip-top freezer bag and freeze for up to 3 months. When you're ready, follow the baking instructions for the recipe. Frozen cookies may need an additional minute or two in the oven.

# CHEWY CHOCOLATE CHIP COOKIES

I prefer the more crisp Classic Chocolate Chip Cookies (page 46), but this recipe is for those of you who, like my dad, prefer a soft, chewy cookie. This is a great recipe with a bit more sugar and some extra flour to get the chewy texture. When you're serving cookies to a crowd, try making both recipes to see which cookie gets more votes.

3 cups [360 g] all-purpose flour

1 tsp baking soda

1 tsp salt

1 cup [220 g] unsalted butter, at room temperature

1 cup [200 g] granulated sugar

1 cup [200 g] firmly packed light brown sugar

2 large eggs

2 tsp vanilla extract

2 cups [340 g] Guittard Semisweet Chocolate Baking Chips

1 cup [110 g] chopped walnuts (optional)

Preheat the oven to 325°F [165°C]. Line two baking sheets with parchment paper.

In a medium bowl, combine the flour, baking soda, and salt. Set aside.

In a large bowl, with a hand mixer, beat together the butter, granulated sugar, and brown sugar until light and smooth, about 3 minutes. Beat in the eggs and vanilla until smooth. Gradually stir in the flour mixture until combined. Fold in the chocolate chips and the walnuts (if using). Drop the dough by rounded tablespoonful onto the prepared baking sheets, leaving 3 in [7.5 cm] between the cookies; the cookies will spread as they bake.

Bake for 14 to 16 minutes, or until light brown around the edges. Cool the cookies on the baking sheet for 2 minutes, before transferring to a wire rack to cool completely. Store in an airtight container at room temperature for up to 1 week.

**MAKES THIRTY 3½-IN [9-CM] COOKIES**

# OATMEAL CHOCOLATE CHIP COOKIES

My friend Hannah loves oatmeal cookies. She'll make a batch of dough, freeze half of it, and then for a few weeks, she'll make freshly baked oatmeal cookies at any hour of the day. Inspired by her love for this hearty (and heart-healthful) cookie, I set out to master a chocolate version. There's a whole range of oatmeal cookies out there, from dense and cakey to delicate and thin. This cookie somehow manages to fall right between those two extremes. A dash of spice and the chocolate chips make them completely irresistible.

**1 cup [120 g] all-purpose flour**

**½ tsp baking soda**

**½ tsp salt**

**½ tsp ground cinnamon**

**¼ tsp ground nutmeg**

**½ cup [110 g] unsalted butter, at room temperature**

**½ cup [100 g] granulated sugar**

**½ cup [100 g] firmly packed light brown sugar**

**1 large egg**

**½ tsp vanilla extract**

**1 cup [170 g] Guittard Semisweet Chocolate Baking Chips**

**¾ cup [60 g] old-fashioned rolled oats**

**½ cup [85 g] dried cherries or cranberries (optional)**

Preheat the oven to 375°F [190°C]. Line two baking sheets with parchment paper.

In a small bowl, combine the flour, baking soda, salt, cinnamon, and nutmeg. Set aside.

In a large bowl, with a hand mixer, beat together the butter, granulated sugar, and brown sugar until light and smooth, about 3 minutes. Beat in the egg and vanilla until smooth. Gradually stir in the flour mixture until combined. Fold in the chocolate chips, rolled oats, and the dried cherries (if using). Drop the dough by rounded tablespoonsful onto the prepared baking sheets, leaving 2 in [5 cm] between the cookies; the cookies will spread as they bake.

Bake for 8 to 10 minutes, or until the edges are set and lightly brown. Transfer the cookies to a wire rack to cool. Store in an airtight container at room temperature for up to 1 week.

**MAKES TWENTY-FOUR 2-IN [5-CM] COOKIES**

# CHOCOLATE MINT CHIP COOKIES

There's something refreshing about the combination of chocolate and mint that leaves my palate feeling perfectly cleansed post dinner. The mint-green chips in these cookies add a festive pop of color to a soft, rich chocolate base. I love making these treats for holiday cookie exchanges. Our recipe uses Guittard Green Mint Baking Chips, but if you can't find them, you can use chopped peppermint sticks or candy canes. The texture will be a bit different but you'll still get the refreshing taste and festive color.

2¼ cups [340 g] Guittard Semisweet Chocolate Baking Wafers

1½ cups [180 g] all-purpose flour

½ tsp baking soda

⅛ tsp salt

½ cup [110 g] unsalted butter, at room temperature

½ cup [100 g] sugar

3 large eggs

2 tsp vanilla extract

2 cups [340 g] Guittard Green Mint Baking Chips

Preheat the oven to 350°F [180°C]. Line two baking sheets with parchment paper.

Melt the chocolate wafers using a hot water bath or the microwave oven (see Note). Stir until completely melted and smooth. Remove the bowl from the water if you used a hot water bath and set aside to cool.

In a small bowl, combine the flour, baking soda, and salt. Set aside.

In a large bowl, with a hand mixer, beat together the butter and sugar until light and fluffy, about 3 minutes. Beat in the cooled melted chocolate, eggs, and vanilla until smooth. Gradually stir in the flour mixture until combined. Fold in the mint chips. Drop the dough by rounded tablespoonsful onto the prepared baking sheets, leaving 2 in [5 cm] between the cookies; the cookies will spread as they bake.

Bake for 8 to 10 minutes, or until the edges are set. Transfer the cookies to a wire rack to cool. Store in an airtight container at room temperature for up to 1 week.

MAKES THIRTY 2-IN [5-CM] COOKIES

NOTE: MELTING CHOCOLATE. You can either set up a hot water bath or melt the chocolate in the microwave oven. Below are instructions for both methods.

*Hot Water Bath*—Fill a medium saucepan with 1 to 2 in [2.5 to 5 cm] of water and bring to a simmer over medium heat. Place the chocolate or chocolate mixture in a heatproof bowl (glass or stainless steel) that will fit on top of the saucepan without touching the water. Set the bowl on top of the saucepan. Remove the bowl from the water and let cool.

*Microwave*—Place the chocolate or chocolate mixture in a medium glass bowl and place in the microwave oven. Microwave in 30-second intervals, stirring well with a rubber spatula after each interval. Stop microwaving when there are still very small lumps in the chocolate and stir until completely smooth. Let cool.

# MACADAMIA NUT WHITE CHOCOLATE CHIP COOKIES

In the early 1930s, my great-grandfather would sail off to Hawaii on the SS *Lurline* to buy macadamia nuts directly from the farmers who grew them. Macadamia nuts and chocolate are one of those exquisite combinations that's hard to pass up. This recipe pairs the crunchiness of the macadamia nut with the creaminess of white chocolate. On the chilliest winter day, these flavors carry a bit of the island's tropical warmth.

**1½ cups [180 g] all-purpose flour**

**½ tsp baking soda**

**½ tsp salt**

**½ cup [110 g] unsalted butter, at room temperature**

**½ cup [100 g] granulated sugar**

**½ cup [100 g] firmly packed light brown sugar**

**1 large egg**

**½ tsp vanilla extract**

**1 cup [170 g] Guittard Choc-Au-Lait Baking Chips (white chocolate)**

**½ cup [55 g] macadamia nuts, halved or chopped**

Preheat the oven to 375°F [190°C]. Line two baking sheets with parchment paper.

In a small bowl, combine the flour, baking soda, and salt. Set aside.

In a large bowl, with a hand mixer, beat together the butter, granulated sugar, and brown sugar until light and smooth, about 3 minutes. Beat in the egg and vanilla until smooth. Gradually stir in the flour mixture until combined. Fold in the white chocolate chips and macadamia nuts. Drop the dough by rounded tablepoonsful onto the prepared baking sheets, leaving 2 in [5 cm] between the cookies; the cookies will spread as they bake.

Bake for 9 to 11 minutes, or until golden brown around the edges. The cookies will be soft but will firm up as they cool. Cool the cookies on the baking sheets for 5 minutes before transferring to a wire rack to cool completely. Store in an airtight container at room temperature for up to 1 week.

**MAKES THIRTY 2½-IN [6-CM] COOKIES**

# PUMPKIN CHOCOLATE CHIP COOKIES

This recipe stands up well to improvisation. I was first inspired by a recipe made by a high school friend, but I have adjusted it numerous times, depending on the occasion and how I was feeling each time I set out to make them. For a 2004 article in the *San Jose Mercury News,* I revised the recipe to include white chocolate chips and oats. Another time, in a fit of delirium, I accidentally made the recipe with buckwheat flour instead of whole-wheat flour, which ended up adding a pleasing extra-hearty flavor. After so many variations over the years, the recipe that appears here has received the stamp of approval from my family. The pumpkin gives these cookies a light and fluffy crumb, like the texture of a muffin. A dash of cinnamon and nutmeg imparts a festive flavor. If you're one of those bakers who likes extra spice, this is a good recipe for you. Just make sure you add a little spice at a time and taste the batter as you go.

1 cup [120 g] all-purpose flour

1¼ cups [150 g] whole-wheat flour

1 tsp baking soda

1 tsp salt

2 tsp ground cinnamon

1 tsp ground nutmeg

4 Tbsp [55 g] unsalted butter, at room temperature

¾ cup [150 g] granulated sugar

¾ cup [150 g] firmly packed light brown sugar

2 large eggs

1 tsp vanilla extract

2 cups [430 g] pumpkin purée

2 cups [340 g] Guittard Semisweet Chocolate Baking Chips

Preheat the oven to 375°F [190°C]. Line two baking sheets with parchment paper.

In a medium bowl, combine the all-purpose flour, whole-wheat flour, baking soda, salt, cinnamon, and nutmeg. Set aside.

CONTINUED

In a large bowl, with a hand mixer, beat together the butter, granulated sugar, and brown sugar until light and smooth, about 3 minutes. Beat in the eggs and vanilla until smooth. Stir in the pumpkin purée until combined. Gradually stir in the flour mixture until combined. Fold in the chocolate chips. Drop the dough by rounded teaspoonsful onto the prepared baking sheets, leaving 1 in [2.5 cm] between the cookies.

Bake for 10 to 12 minutes, or until the cookies are firm and spring back when touched. Transfer the cookies to a wire rack to cool. Store in an airtight container at room temperature for up to 1 week.

**MAKES FORTY-FIVE 2-IN [5-CM] COOKIES**

# MOCHA COOKIES

We Guittards do like our chocolate, but we're also a big coffee-loving family. I have what I like to call a manageable addiction (three cups of coffee a day seems about right). Combine that with my craving for sweets, and you can see why a mocha cookie is so appealing. Like any good mocha, this cookie combines a generous dose of chocolate with a blast of espresso. When you're looking for an afternoon pick-me-up, this is a perfect option. To add another hit of flavor, chop up chunks of dark chocolate and stir them into the cookie dough just before baking. You can find espresso powder at most gourmet food stores or you can purchase it online.

**1¾ cups [255 g] Guittard Semisweet or Bittersweet Chocolate Baking Wafers**

**1 cup [120 g] all-purpose flour**

**¼ cup [20 g] Guittard Cocoa Rouge (Dutch-processed unsweetened cocoa powder)**

**2 tsp baking powder**

**¼ tsp salt**

**1½ tsp espresso powder**

**½ cup [110 g] unsalted butter, at room temperature**

**1 cup [200 g] sugar**

**2 large eggs**

**1 tsp vanilla extract**

Preheat the oven to 350°F [180°C]. Line two baking sheets with parchment paper.

Melt the chocolate wafers using a hot water bath or the microwave oven (see Note: Melting Chocolate, page 51). Stir until completely melted and smooth. Remove the bowl from the water if you used a hot water bath and set aside to cool.

In a small bowl, combine the flour, cocoa powder, baking powder, salt, and espresso powder. Set aside.

In a large bowl, with a hand mixer, beat together the butter and sugar until light and fluffy, about 3 minutes. Beat in the eggs, one at a time; add the vanilla; and beat until smooth. Stir in the cooled melted chocolate until well combined. Gradually stir in the flour mixture until combined. Drop the dough by rounded teaspoonful onto the prepared baking sheets, leaving 2 in [5 cm] between the cookies; the cookies will spread as they bake.

Bake for 7 to 9 minutes, until the sides are slightly cracked and the centers are still unset and gooey. Cool the cookies on the baking sheets for about 3 minutes before transferring to a wire rack to cool completely. Store in an airtight container at room temperature for up to 1 week.

**MAKES TWENTY-EIGHT 2½-IN [6-CM] COOKIES**

# MOLTEN CHOCOLATE COOKIES

When you need to slow down, sip a latte, and read a book, this is the cookie you'll want on a pretty plate beside you. They're big (only eight cookies per baking sheet!) and very rich, with a crisp exterior and gooey center—everything you want from a chocolate indulgence. I'll whip up a batch and keep some dough in the freezer for those moments that require something special (or when a serious chocolate craving hits). Be careful not to overcook these or you won't get the fudgy middle. If you leave the dough in the refrigerator overnight, put it on the counter and let it sit at room temperature for 20 minutes before baking.

**2¼ cups [340 g] Guittard Semisweet Chocolate Baking Wafers**

**3 Tbsp unsalted butter, at room temperature**

**1 cup [120 g] all-purpose flour**

**½ tsp baking powder**

**½ tsp salt**

**2 large eggs**

**½ cup [100 g] sugar**

**1 tsp vanilla extract**

Preheat the oven to 375°F [190°C]. Line two baking sheets with parchment paper.

Melt the chocolate wafers and butter together using a hot water bath or the microwave oven (see Note: Melting Chocolate, page 51). Stir until completely melted and smooth. Remove the bowl from the water if you used a hot water bath and set aside to cool.

In a small bowl, combine the flour, baking powder, and salt. Set aside.

In a large bowl, with a hand mixer, beat together the eggs, sugar, and vanilla until pale yellow and slightly thickened, 2 to 3 minutes. Stir in the cooled melted chocolate mixture. Gradually stir in the flour mixture until just incorporated. Cover the dough with plastic wrap and refrigerate for at least 15 minutes, or up to overnight.

CONTINUED

Scoop 2-in [5-cm] mounds onto the prepared baking sheets, leaving 2 in [5 cm] between the cookies; the cookies will spread as they bake.

Bake for 12 minutes, or until crusty on the outside but soft in the center. Leave the cookies on the baking sheet for 3 to 5 minutes to firm up, then serve immediately. Store in an airtight container at room temperature for up to 1 week. Reheat to achieve the molten chocolate gooeyness by microwaving them for 10 seconds.

**MAKES SIXTEEN 3-IN [7.5-CM] COOKIES**

# PEANUT BUTTER DARK CHOCOLATE THUMBPRINT COOKIES

What makes the peanut butter–chocolate combination so irresistible? Perhaps it's the blend of sweet and salty. Or maybe it's the play on textures—melted chocolate with softly whipped peanut butter. This thumbprint cookie celebrates everything that's good about the classic PB-DC combination. One bite takes me back to Saturday mornings with the Muppets (yup, my brother and I were allowed to eat cookies for breakfast; lucky ducks, I know). Peanut butter and dark chocolate: always a win, any time of day.

**COOKIES**

1¼ cups [150 g] all-purpose flour

¾ tsp baking soda

½ tsp baking powder

¼ tsp salt

½ cup [110 g] unsalted butter, at room temperature

½ cup [100 g] granulated sugar

½ cup [100 g] firmly packed dark brown sugar

½ cup [125 g] crunchy peanut butter

1 large egg, lightly beaten

1 tsp vanilla extract

**FILLING**

2 oz [50 g] Guittard Bittersweet Chocolate Baking Bar, broken into small pieces

2 Tbsp unsalted butter, at room temperature

¾ tsp light corn syrup

**To make the cookies:** Preheat the oven to 350°F [180°C]. Line two baking sheets with parchment paper.

In a small bowl, combine the flour, baking soda, baking powder, and salt. Set aside.

In a large bowl, with a hand mixer, beat together the butter, granulated sugar, and brown sugar until light and fluffy, about 3 minutes. Stir in the peanut butter, egg, and vanilla. Gradually stir in the flour mixture until combined.

Roll pieces of dough into 1-in [2.5-cm] balls and place on the prepared baking sheets about 1 in [2.5 cm] apart.

CONTINUED

Bake for 10 minutes, then remove from the oven. Using a small spoon, make a small indentation in the middle of each cookie. Return the cookies to the oven for another 6 to 7 minutes, or until set. (After removing from the oven, you may need to use the spoon again to make the indentations clear.) Transfer the cookies to a wire rack to cool completely, 1 to 2 hours.

**To make the filling:** Melt the chocolate, butter, and corn syrup together using a hot water bath or the microwave oven (see Note: Melting Chocolate, page 51). Stir until completely melted and smooth. Remove the bowl from the water if you used a hot water bath and set aside to cool slightly, 3 to 5 minutes.

When the cookies are completely cool, use a spoon to fill each indentation with the chocolate filling. Set aside and let the chocolate filling cool and harden, 1 to 2 hours. (If your kitchen is warm, refrigerate the cookies so the filling can harden.) Store in an airtight container at room temperature for up to 1 week.

**MAKES TWENTY-FOUR 1-IN [2.5-CM] COOKIES**

# YO YOS

If you're not yet familiar with Yo Yos (otherwise known as Whoopie Pies, Black Moons, Gobs, or BFOs), you're in for a real treat. Yo Yos yield a perfect cake-to-frosting ratio in an easy-to-devour format. A classic buttercream with a dash of lemon zest goes perfectly with the chocolate, offering a clean, crisp flavor complement to the dark, rich cake. If you're looking for a chocolate dessert for a summer picnic, this is it. Really love buttercream? Double the recipe and add as much filling as your heart desires.

**COOKIES**

¾ cup [70 g] Guittard Cocoa Rouge (Dutch-processed unsweetened cocoa powder)

2 cups [240 g] all-purpose flour

½ tsp baking powder

½ tsp baking soda

½ tsp salt

¼ cup [55 g] unsalted butter, at room temperature

1 cup [200 g] firmly packed light brown sugar

1 large egg

1 tsp vanilla extract

1 cup [240 ml] full-fat buttermilk

**LEMON BUTTERCREAM**

½ cup [110 g] unsalted butter, at room temperature

1⅓ cups [160 g] confectioners' sugar

2 tsp whole milk

1 tsp vanilla extract

1 tsp grated lemon zest

CONTINUED

**To make the cookies:** Preheat the oven to 350°F [180°C]. Line two baking sheets with parchment paper.

In a medium bowl, whisk together the cocoa powder, flour, baking powder, baking soda, and salt. Set aside.

In a large bowl, with a hand mixer, beat together the butter and brown sugar until light and fluffy, about 3 minutes. Beat in the egg and vanilla until well combined. Alternately add the flour mixture and the buttermilk in four additions, beating on low speed until smooth and stopping to scrape down the bowl after each addition. Drop the dough by teaspoonful onto the prepared baking sheets, leaving 2 in [5 cm] between the cookies; the cookies will spread as they bake. Make an even number of cookies, if you can, so you can sandwich them together.

Bake for 9 to 11 minutes, or until domed with a center that springs back when lightly tapped. Cool the cookies on the baking sheets for 5 minutes before transferring to a wire rack to cool completely. (At this point, you can freeze the cookies for up to 2 months.)

**To make the lemon buttercream:** In a medium bowl, using a hand mixer, beat together the butter and confectioners' sugar until light and fluffy. Beat in the milk and vanilla until the buttercream is thick. Add the lemon zest and beat until combined.

Spread about 1 Tbsp buttercream onto the flat side of a cookie. Top with a cookie of similar size, flat-side down, to sandwich together. Repeat until all of the cookies are sandwiched. Let the Yo Yos sit at room temperature for 30 minutes to 1 hour before serving so the buttercream can set. Store in an airtight container in the refrigerator for up to 4 days.

**MAKES TWENTY-FIVE 1½-IN [4-CM] SANDWICH COOKIES**

# CHOCOLATE PISTACHIO SABLÉS

I often pick flavor combinations based on taste rather than aesthetics, so it's an extra bonus when the ingredient pairing is as pretty as it is in this cookie. Because this is a slice-and-bake cookie, you can freeze the dough, if wrapped airtight, for up to two months. You don't even need to defrost before slicing and baking, which means you can produce a spontaneous midnight snack that's as easy as it is impressive.

**1 cup [120 g] all-purpose flour**

**½ cup [60 g] light rye flour**

**½ tsp baking soda**

**½ tsp baking powder**

**¼ tsp salt**

**½ cup [50 g] Guittard Cocoa Rouge (Dutch-processed unsweetened cocoa powder)**

**½ cup [55 g] butter, at room temperature**

**¾ cup [150 g] firmly packed light brown sugar**

**2 egg yolks**

**1 tsp vanilla extract**

**½ cup [60 g] shelled, chopped unsalted pistachio nuts**

**Fleur de sel for sprinkling**

In a medium bowl, combine the all-purpose flour, light rye flour, baking soda, baking powder, salt, and cocoa powder. Set aside.

In a large bowl, with a hand mixer, beat together the butter and brown sugar until light and fluffy, about 3 minutes. Beat in the egg yolks, one at a time, and the vanilla. Gradually stir in the flour mixture until combined. Fold in the pistachios.

Divide the dough in half. Roll each half into a log, about 2 in [5 cm] wide by 10 in [25 cm] long. Wrap the logs tightly in plastic wrap and refrigerate for at least 30 minutes, or freeze for up to 2 months.

Preheat the oven to 350°F [180°C]. Line two baking sheets with parchment paper.

Remove the dough from the refrigerator. (If the dough has been in the freezer, let it sit at room temperature for 15 minutes.) Unwrap the dough and cut it into ½-in [12-mm] slices. Set the dough slices on the prepared baking sheets, leaving 1 in [2.5 cm] between the cookies. Sprinkle each cookie with fleur de sel.

Bake for 11 to 13 minutes, or until the centers appear set. Transfer the cookies to a wire rack and let cool for 10 minutes. Store in an airtight container at room temperature for up to 1 week.

**MAKES TWENTY-FIVE 2-IN [5-CM] COOKIES**

# SALTED CHOCOLATE SHORTBREAD

My friend Ben harvests sea salt on the Oregon coast. He traipses knee-deep out into the chilly Pacific Ocean to gather buckets of water and then he carries the salt water home, where time and heat will work their slow magic. The result? Beautifully intricate flakes of sea salt. As with anything you cook or bake, using good ingredients is crucial, even if that ingredient has just a small role in the final product. Everything from the cacao beans we purchase down to the fleur de sel sprinkled on top of these cookies are top quality, which is what makes this recipe so good. The Cocoa Rouge adds richness to this shortbread, and the buttery yet crunchy texture can satisfy a craving at any time of day.

**1¼ cups [150 g] all-purpose flour**

**⅓ cup [35 g] Guittard Cocoa Rouge (Dutch-processed unsweetened cocoa powder)**

**½ tsp baking soda**

**½ tsp salt**

**¾ cup [170 g] unsalted butter, at room temperature**

**¼ cup [50 g] granulated sugar**

**½ cup [100 g] firmly packed dark brown sugar**

**¾ tsp vanilla extract**

**Fleur de sel for sprinkling**

Preheat the oven to 350°F [180°C]. Line two baking sheets with parchment paper.

In a small bowl, combine the flour, cocoa powder, baking soda, and salt. Set aside.

In a large bowl, using a hand mixer, beat together the butter, granulated sugar, brown sugar, and vanilla until light and smooth, about 3 minutes. Gradually stir in the flour mixture until combined. Roll the dough into 1½-in [4-cm] balls and set them on the prepared baking sheets, leaving 1 in [2.5 cm] between the balls. Use the bottom of a flat cup to slightly flatten each ball, and then sprinkle the balls with fleur de sel.

Bake for 13 to 15 minutes, or until the tops are cracked. Transfer the cookies to a wire rack to cool. Store in an airtight container at room temperature for up to 1 week.

**MAKES TWENTY-EIGHT 2-IN [5-CM] COOKIES**

# CHOCOLATE MERINGUES

My great-aunt Camille, who wrote a column for the *San Francisco Chronicle* called "Camille's Corner," was famous for two recipes: her Chipped Beef in Sour Cream and her Chocolate Meringues—a French-style egg white "cookie" with a light and airy texture. Camille's daughter, Mimi, who watched her mom bake these time and time again, always reminds me that whatever you do, don't open the oven door while the meringues are baking. Cool air can cause the air bubbles in the batter to move and shift, resulting in misshapen meringues. I like to use one of my favorite single-origin chocolate bars for this recipe: Sur del Lago bittersweet from Venezuela.

**2 oz [60 g] Guittard Sur del Lago Venezuela (65% cacao) Bittersweet Chocolate Bar**

**2 egg whites, at room temperature**

**½ cup [100 g] superfine sugar**

Preheat the oven to 250°F [120°C]. Line two baking sheets with parchment paper.

Using a box grater or vegetable peeler, slice the chocolate very thinly. (You may need to start and stop this a few times because your warm hands will begin to melt the chocolate bar, making the grating or peeling difficult.) Set aside.

In the clean, dry bowl of a stand mixer fitted with the whisk attachment (or in a large bowl using a hand mixer fitted with whisk beaters), beat the egg whites on low speed until frothy (you will see small bubbles start to form), about 1 minute, then increase the speed to medium-high and beat until stiff peaks form when you lift the beaters, 4 to 6 minutes. Turn the speed to low and gradually add the sugar, 1 Tbsp at a time. You'll know the meringue mixture is ready when you pull the whisk attachment out of the bowl and the meringue hangs on to the whisk and holds its shape. Gently fold in the chocolate curls using a rubber spatula, being careful not to overmix so the meringue won't collapse.

Drop the meringues by small teaspoonsful onto the prepared baking sheets.

CONTINUED

Bake for 50 minutes, or until you can lift the meringues off the parchment without them sticking. Let the meringues cool completely on the baking sheet. Store in an airtight container at room temperature for up to 1 week.

**MAKES TWENTY-SIX 1½-IN [4-CM] MERINGUES**

**NOTE:** You can choose to bake meringues over-night in a low oven. This is a nice way to go during warmer months. Preheat the oven to 200°F [95°C]. Prepare the meringues as directed and put them in the oven. After 10 minutes, turn off the oven and leave the meringues in the oven overnight. Make sure you do not open the oven.

# CHOCOLATE CHEWS

My sister-in-law Alice has a slight obsession with everything related to tea. She's very persuasive in coaxing the rest of us to slow down and enjoy the ritual of making and sharing a pot of tea. These pop-in-your-mouth treats are just right when you'd like a small, tasty bite to accompany a hot cup and a good conversation.

**2¼ cups [340 g] Guittard Semisweet Chocolate Baking Wafers**

**2 cups [240 g] all-purpose flour**

**½ tsp baking soda**

**½ tsp baking powder**

**¼ tsp salt**

**½ cup [110 g] unsalted butter, at room temperature**

**1¼ cups [250 g] sugar**

**2 large eggs**

Preheat the oven to 350°F [180°C]. Line two baking sheets with parchment paper.

Melt the chocolate wafers using a hot water bath or the microwave oven (see Note: Melting Chocolate, page 51). Stir until completely melted and smooth. Remove the bowl from the water if you used a hot water bath and set aside to cool.

In a small bowl, combine the flour, baking soda, baking powder, and salt. Set aside.

In a large bowl, with a hand mixer, beat together the butter and 1 cup [200 g] of the sugar until light and fluffy, about 3 minutes. Beat in the eggs, one at a time. Add the cooled melted chocolate and stir to combine. Gradually stir in the flour mixture until combined.

Put the remaining ¼ cup [50 g] sugar in a small, shallow dish. Roll the dough into 1-in [2.5-cm] balls, then roll the balls in the sugar to coat them. Place the balls on the prepared baking sheets, leaving 2 in [5 cm] between the cookies; the cookies will spread as they bake.

Bake for 10 to 12 minutes, or until the tops are cracked and the centers are still soft. Let the cookies cool on the baking sheets for 2 to 3 minutes before transferring to a wire rack to cool completely. Store in an airtight container at room temperature for up to 1 week.

**MAKES FIFTY 2-IN [5-CM] COOKIES**

# HOT COCOA MADELEINES

Madeleines are my favorite cookie. I love their delicate flavor, distinctive shape, and texture—they taste more like a mini sponge cake than a cookie. When I was a kid, my mom would take me to a coffee shop a few blocks from our house. She'd get her latte and I'd get hot chocolate and a madeleine pulled from an old-fashioned lidded candy jar that sat on the counter. As we sipped our drinks, I'd nibble off the golden-brown edges in an attempt to make the cookie last as long as possible. I don't think I'll ever fall out of love with them.

This recipe uses our rich drinking chocolate to produce a rich chocolatey version of the traditional madeleine.

⅔ cup [80 g] all-purpose flour

3 Tbsp Guittard Grand Cacao Drinking Chocolate (sweet ground cocoa)

½ tsp baking powder

Pinch of salt

2 large eggs

½ cup [100 g] sugar

1 tsp vanilla extract

6 Tbsp [85 g] unsalted butter, melted and cooled

Confectioners' sugar for dusting (optional)

In a small bowl, whisk together the flour, hot chocolate mix, baking powder, and salt. Set aside.

In the bowl of a stand mixer fitted with the whisk attachment (or in a large bowl using a hand mixer fitted with whisk beaters), beat the eggs on low speed for 1 minute, then increase the speed to medium-high and gradually beat in the sugar. Continue beating for 2 to 3 minutes until soft peaks form. Add the vanilla and beat on low speed until combined. Using a rubber spatula, fold in the flour mixture until just combined, then fold in the melted butter until just combined. Cover with plastic wrap, placing the plastic wrap directly on the surface of the batter. Place the bowl in the refrigerator to rest for 3 hours, or up to overnight.

Preheat the oven to 375°F [190°C]. If you have a nonstick madeleine pan, lightly butter the pan. If you have a madeleine pan that is tin or made from another metal, butter and flour the pan. If you have a silicone madeleine mold, you don't need to butter or flour the mold.

Remove the batter from the refrigerator. Spoon teaspoonsful of batter into the madeleine pan molds, filling them almost to the top.

Bake for 9 to 11 minutes, or until the madeleines are lightly puffed in the middle and the tops spring back after a light tap. Remove the madeleines from the oven. As soon as the madeleines are cool enough to touch, remove them from the pan and place them on a wire rack. (If after 2 minutes the cookies are still too hot, use a butter knife to gently pop them out.) When completely cool, lightly dust each cookie with confectioners' sugar (if desired). Store in an airtight container at room temperature for up to 4 days; or in an airtight zip-top bag in the freezer for up to 2 months.

**MAKES TWENTY COOKIES**

# CHOCOLATE-HAZELNUT MACARONS

The macaron is a cookie for which Paris is renowned. It's a delicate, light confection in which flavored ganache is sandwiched between two small cookies made of almond flour. (A macaron is not to be confused with a macaroon, which is a rounded coconut cookie.) If any recipe has the potential to transport you to Paris, it's this one. Perhaps it's the cookie's delicate texture, which melts as soon as it hits your tongue, or the balanced sweetness you taste with every bite. Whatever it is, you'll be right there, sitting in a Luxembourg chair at the Jardin des Tuilleries.

Macarons can be finicky, so don't get frustrated if the first attempt doesn't yield the perfect confection you buy from a bakery. A few tips if you're a first-time macaron baker: Use aged egg whites (crack them and leave them exposed for a day or two). This allows for the water of the egg whites to evaporate, making them slightly more acidic, and strengthens the egg white protein, giving you a stronger meringue when whipped. Once you've piped the batter onto the baking sheets, lightly rap the baking sheets against the counter just before putting them in the oven, to ensure that you get those famous macaron "feet."

## MACARONS

1 cup [100 g] confectioners' sugar

¼ cup [30 g] almond flour

¼ cup [30 g] hazelnut flour

2 Tbsp Guittard Cocoa Rouge (Dutch-processed unsweetened cocoa powder)

2 egg whites, at room temperature

5 Tbsp [55 g] superfine sugar

## GANACHE

6 oz [170 g] Guittard Semisweet Chocolate Baking Bars, broken into small pieces

½ cup [120 ml] heavy whipping cream

2 Tbsp light corn syrup

6 Tbsp [85 g] unsalted butter, at room temperature

**To make the macarons:** Preheat the oven to 350°F [180°C]. Line two baking sheets with parchment paper (or Silpat baking mats, if you have them). Fit a large pastry bag with a ½-in [12-mm] plain tip (or set a 1-gl [3.75-L] zip-top bag inside a large cup or small bowl so it's standing up).

Using a food processor, blend together the confectioners' sugar, almond flour, hazelnut flour, and cocoa powder until fine and combined, about 30 seconds.

In the clean, dry bowl of a stand mixer fitted with the whisk attachment (or in a large bowl using a hand mixer fitted with whisk beaters), beat the egg whites on low speed until frothy (you will see small bubbles start to form), about 1 minute, then increase the speed to medium-high and beat until soft peaks form. Gradually add the superfine sugar and beat until firm peaks form, 3 to 4 minutes.

Using a rubber spatula, gently fold the flour mixture into the egg white mixture in four additions until just combined. With the final addition, stop folding when there are no more traces of the egg white, being careful not to overmix.

Transfer the batter to the pastry bag or zip-top bag. (If using a zip-top bag, push all the batter toward one bottom corner, cut off the opposite bottom corner of the bag and, pushing out all of the air from the bag, squeeze the batter toward the hole.) Slowly pipe 1-in [2.5-cm] rounds about 1 in [2.5 cm] apart onto the prepared baking sheets. After piping all the rounds, hold a baking sheet by the edges and rap it against the counter to help create the macaron feet, and repeat with the other baking sheet.

Bake for 14 to 16 minutes, or until the tops are domed and firm. Transfer the macarons to a wire rack to cool completely, about 1 hour.

**To make the ganache:** Place the chocolate in a medium bowl. Set aside.

In a medium saucepan, bring the cream and corn syrup just to a boil, stirring frequently. Pour the hot cream mixture over the chocolate. Let the chocolate mixture stand for 3 minutes, then stir with a rubber spatula. Add the butter and stir until combined. Pour the ganache into a shallow glass baking dish and allow it to set at room temperature for 1 hour or until it is spreadable. (The ganache can be stored at room temperature in an airtight container for 1 day.)

Find two cookies that are approximately the same size. Spread 1 Tbsp of ganache on the flat side of one cookie. Place the second cookie on top of the ganache, flat-side down. Press down gently on the cookie sandwich, and put on a wire rack or plate. Repeat until you have filled all the macarons. Let them rest for at least 30 minutes so the ganache can set. Store in an airtight container at room temperature for up to 3 days.

**MAKES TWENTY-FIVE MACARONS**

# SIERRA NUGGETS

I like these hearty cookies in part because they remind me of the people who flooded into California in the 1800s in search of gold, including my great-great-grandfather Etienne. These nuggets are packed full of energy-sustaining ingredients— nuts, cornflakes, oats, and coconut—as well as a variety of fragrant spices. They make for an unexpectedly delicious treat. Eureka!

1½ cups [180 g] all-purpose flour

1¼ tsp baking soda

1 tsp salt

1½ tsp ground cinnamon

½ tsp ground mace

¼ tsp ground nutmeg

⅛ tsp ground cloves

1 cup [110 g] unsalted butter, at room temperature

1½ cups [300 g] granulated sugar

1 cup [200 g] firmly packed dark brown sugar

3 Tbsp whole milk

1½ tsp vanilla extract

2 large eggs, lightly beaten

1 cup [25 g] cornflakes

3 cups [240 g] old-fashioned rolled oats

1 cup [90 g] unsweetened shredded coconut

2 cups [340 g] Guittard Milk Chocolate Baking Chips or Guittard Semisweet Chocolate Baking Chips

1 cup [110 g] pine nuts, peanuts, or chopped walnuts

Preheat the oven to 350°F [180°C]. Line two baking sheets with parchment paper.

In a medium bowl, combine the flour, baking soda, salt, cinnamon, mace, nutmeg, and cloves. Set aside.

In a large bowl, using a hand mixer, beat together the butter, granulated sugar, and brown sugar until smooth. Beat in the milk, vanilla, and eggs until well combined. One item at a time, stir in the cornflakes, oats, flour mixture, coconut, chocolate chips, and nuts until each addition is just incorporated. Drop the dough by well-rounded teaspoonful onto the prepared baking sheets about 1 in [2.5 cm] apart.

Bake for 9 to 11 minutes, or until the tops are crisp. Let the cookies sit for 2 minutes before removing them from the baking sheets. Store in an airtight container at room temperature for up to 1 week.

**MAKES FORTY-EIGHT 2-IN [5-CM] COOKIES**

*Chapter 3*

# BROWNIES & BARS

# DECADENT BROWNIES

When this brownie first appeared on my desk, its gloriously dense texture and rich chocolate color called out to me. It was love at first bite. We made a few tweaks to the recipe (we dialed back the butter, which you'd never guess if I hadn't told you), and voilà, you've got the best darn brownie recipe at your fingertips. Don't forget to lick the bowl and the spoon.

**6 oz [170 g] Guittard Unsweetened Chocolate Baking Bars, broken into small pieces**

**1 cup plus 2 Tbsp [250 g] unsalted butter, at room temperature**

**4 large eggs**

**2½ cups [500 g] sugar**

**1 tsp vanilla extract**

**1 tsp salt**

**1¾ cups [210 g] all-purpose flour**

Preheat the oven to 350°F [180°C]. Line a 9-by-9-by-2-in [23-by-23-by-5-cm] baking pan with aluminum foil, covering the bottom, up the sides, and hanging about 1 in [2.5 cm] over the sides.

Melt the chocolate and butter together using a hot water bath or the microwave oven (see Note: Melting Chocolate, page 51). Stir until completely melted and smooth. Remove the bowl from the water if you used a hot water bath and set aside to cool.

In a large bowl, with a hand mixer, beat together the eggs, sugar, vanilla, and salt on high speed until light and creamy, 2 to 3 minutes. Blend in the cooled melted chocolate mixture on low speed. Gradually beat in the flour until just incorporated. Spread the batter evenly in the prepared pan.

Bake for 40 to 50 minutes, or until the top is puffed and cracked. Don't overbake; these brownies set as they cool. Let cool completely in the pan. When ready to serve, carefully use the foil to lift the brownies out of the pan. Place the brownies on a cutting board, discard the foil, and cut them into 2-in [5-cm] squares. Store wrapped tightly in plastic wrap at room temperature for up to 1 week. To freeze, cut into four large sections and remove from the pan. Wrap the sections tightly in plastic wrap. Place the sections in a zip-top freezer bag and push out all the air. Freeze for up to 1 month. Let the wrapped sections defrost in the refrigerator overnight.

**MAKES SIXTEEN 2-IN [5-CM] BROWNIES**

# CLOUD NINE BROWNIES

These heavenly brownies are made from a winning combo of three different kinds of chocolate: white, milk, and semisweet. My older brother, Jesse, used to bake these brownies when we were kids. He wasn't the tidiest baker—he'd strew flour, sugar, and eggshells across the countertop, yet he managed to make an irresistibly delicious brownie every time. These were the first treats Jesse learned to bake and, to this day, they remain one of his favorites to whip up. Now, every time I hear someone say, "I'm on Cloud Nine," I think of Jesse, these addictive squares, and the "cloud nine" feeling you get when they melt in your mouth.

**1½ cups [255 g] Guittard Choc-Au-Lait Baking Chips (white chocolate)**

**6 Tbsp [85 g] unsalted butter, cut into small cubes**

**2 large eggs**

**½ cup [100 g] sugar**

**1 tsp vanilla extract**

**¼ tsp salt**

**1 cup [120 g] all-purpose flour**

**½ cup [85 g] Guittard Milk Chocolate Baking Chips**

**½ cup [85 g] Guittard Semisweet Chocolate Baking Chips**

Preheat the oven to 325°F [165°C]. Line an 8-in [20-cm] square pan with aluminum foil, covering the bottom, up the sides, and hanging about 1 in [2.5 cm] over the sides.

Melt 1 cup [170 g] of the white chocolate chips and the butter together using a hot water bath or the microwave oven (see Note: Melting Chocolate, page 51). Stir until completely melted and smooth. Remove the bowl from the water if you used a hot water bath and set aside to cool.

In a large bowl, with a hand mixer, beat together the eggs, sugar, vanilla, and salt on high speed until very pale and thick, 2 to 3 minutes. Blend in the cooled melted white chocolate mixture on low speed. Gradually beat in the flour until just combined. With a wooden spoon, fold in the remaining ½ cup [85 g] white chocolate chips, the milk chocolate chips, and semisweet chocolate chips. Spread the batter evenly in the prepared pan.

Bake for 35 to 40 minutes, or until a toothpick inserted into the center comes out almost clean. Let cool in the pan overnight so the chocolate can set. When ready to serve, carefully use the foil to lift the brownies out of the pan. Place the brownies on a cutting board, discard the foil, and cut them into 1½-in [4-cm] squares. Store in an airtight container at room temperature for up to 1 week. To freeze, cut into four large sections and remove from the pan. Wrap the sections tightly in plastic wrap. Place the sections in a zip-top freezer bag and push out all the air. Freeze for up to 1 month. Let the wrapped sections defrost in the refrigerator overnight.

**MAKES THIRTY-SIX 1½-IN [4-CM] BROWNIES**

# COCOA BROWNIES

For a fudgier brownie, you start with a pot of melted chocolate (see Decadent Brownies, page 82). For a cakier brownie, you use cocoa powder. You might be wondering how cocoa powder can result in a brownie that's as delicious as one made with melted chocolate, but it does. In fact, it was my grandfather's favorite. Here's the secret: Dutch-processed cocoa powder gives a familiar chocolate flavor, sometimes referred to as that nostalgic "Oreo cookie" flavor. The cocoa powder used in this recipe, Cocoa Rouge, has a distinct mahogany color that gives the brownies a beautiful red tone. Brownies made with Cocoa Rouge will be moist, soft, and intensely choco-latey. This brownie is perfect for an afternoon snack or as the base for a brownie sundae.

1¼ cups [150 g] all-purpose flour

1¼ cups [120 g] Guittard Cocoa Rouge (Dutch-processed unsweetened cocoa powder)

½ tsp salt

1½ cups [330 g] unsalted butter, melted and cooled

3 cups [600 g] sugar

7 large eggs

2 tsp vanilla extract

2 cups [220 g] chopped walnuts (optional)

Preheat the oven to 350°F [180°C]. Line a 9-by-13-by-2-in [23-by-33-by-5-cm] baking pan with aluminum foil, covering the bottom, up the sides, and hanging about 1 in [2.5 cm] over the sides.

In a medium bowl, combine the flour, cocoa powder, and salt. Set aside.

In a large bowl, with a hand mixer, beat together the butter and sugar on high speed until light and fluffy, about 3 minutes. Beat in the eggs, one at a time, until smooth and glossy. Mix in the vanilla. Gradually beat in the flour mixture until smooth and free of lumps. Stir in the walnuts (if using). Spread the batter evenly into the pre-pared pan.

Bake for 45 to 50 minutes, or until a toothpick inserted into the center comes out bearing some moist crumbs. Let cool completely in the pan on a wire rack. When ready to serve, carefully use the foil to lift the brownies out of the pan. Place the brownies on a cutting board, discard the foil, and cut them into 2-in [5-cm] squares. Store wrapped tightly in plastic wrap at room temperature for up to 1 week. To freeze, cut into four large sections and remove from the pan. Wrap the sections tightly in plastic wrap. Place the sections in a zip-top freezer bag and push out all the air. Freeze for up to 1 month. Let the wrapped sections defrost in the refrigerator overnight.

**MAKES TWENTY-FOUR 2-IN [5-CM] BROWNIES**

# CHOCOLATE BANANA BLONDIES

These are not your average blondie. In fact, they're not your average anything. One of our newer recipes, these have become a fan favorite around the office and have proven to be completely addictive and irresistible. What makes a blondie a blondie? They don't have the chocolate base you'd find in a brownie but instead start with butter and brown sugar. What makes this blondie extraordinary is that its layers keep getting more intense with every bite. The chocolate crust. The nutty filling. The dash of bourbon, the subtle banana flavor, and the crunch from the cacao nibs carry this treat over the top.

**CRUST**

3 cups [200 g] chocolate wafer cookies

½ cup [110 g] unsalted butter, melted

¼ cup [50 g] firmly packed dark brown sugar

Pinch of salt

**FILLING**

¾ cup [165 g] unsalted butter, at room temperature

1 cup [120 g] all-purpose flour

½ tsp salt

2 Tbsp Guittard Cocoa Rouge (Dutch-processed unsweetened cocoa powder)

2 ripe medium bananas, mashed

2 Tbsp bourbon

2 large eggs

1 tsp vanilla extract

2½ cups [500 g] firmly packed dark brown sugar

½ cup [55 g] toasted walnuts, chopped (see Note)

1 Tbsp cacao nibs

Fleur de sel for sprinkling

CONTINUED

**To make the crust:** Preheat the oven to 375°F [190°C]. Butter a sheet of parchment paper, then use it, butter-side up, to line a 9-by-13-by-2-in [23-by-33-by-5-cm] baking pan.

Using a food processor, pulse the chocolate wafer cookies to fine crumbs. Add the melted butter, brown sugar, and salt. Process until the mixture is the consistency of wet sand. Pour the crumb mixture into the prepared pan and use your fingers to push the mixture down and spread it evenly over the bottom of the pan to form a crust.

Bake for 7 to 10 minutes, until set. Remove the pan from the oven and set on a wire rack to cool.

**To make the filling:** Lower the oven temperature to 350°F [180°C].

In a medium saucepan, melt the butter over low heat. Let the butter cook until the foam subsides and the butter turns brown, about 5 minutes. Set aside.

In a small bowl, combine the flour, salt, and cocoa powder. Set aside.

In a large bowl, with a hand mixer, beat together the bananas, bourbon, eggs, vanilla, and brown sugar. Beat in the brown butter until combined. Fold in the flour mixture and walnuts.

Pour the filling over the cooked crust and spread it evenly. Sprinkle with the cacao nibs and fleur de sel.

Bake for 45 to 55 minutes, or until a toothpick inserted into the center comes out clean. Let cool completely in the pan. When ready to serve, invert the pan on a cutting board and rap the pan on the surface until the blondies release from the pan. Peel away the parchment and discard. Cut into 3-in [7.5-cm] squares. Store wrapped tightly in plastic wrap at room temperature for up to 5 days. To freeze, cut into four large sections and remove from the pan. Wrap the sections tightly in plastic wrap. Place the sections in a zip-top freezer bag and push out all the air. Freeze for up to 1 month. Let the wrapped sections defrost in the refrigerator overnight.

**MAKES TWELVE 3-IN [7.5-CM] BARS**

**NOTE:** TOASTING NUTS. Preheat the oven to 350°F [180°C]. Line a baking sheet with parchment paper, spread the nuts out on the parchment paper, and bake for 8 to 10 minutes, until you smell the nuts toasting and they have slightly darkened in color. Be sure to check on the nuts often while they are toasting, because they burn easily.

# TREAT BARS

When you're in the mood for the flavor of chocolate chip cookies but you don't have time to dish out spoonfuls of dough, bars are the way to go. Bars give you everything you love in a cookie along with a whole bunch of crunchy, chewy edges. Plus, they're easy and quick to make. This recipe is a basic cookie bar with nuts and chocolate. It's simple enough that you might even be able to commit the recipe to memory. Try different nut and chocolate combinations each time you make them. For picnics or trips to the beach, just leave the bars in the pan and go.

**1¼ cups [150 g] all-purpose flour**

**½ tsp baking soda**

**¼ tsp salt**

**½ cup [110 g] unsalted butter, at room temperature**

**¼ cup [50 g] granulated sugar**

**½ cup [100 g] firmly packed light brown sugar**

**1 large egg**

**½ tsp vanilla extract**

**½ cup [55 g] walnuts, chopped**

**1½ cups [255 g] Guittard Semisweet Chocolate Baking Chips**

Preheat the oven to 350°F [180°C]. Lightly butter a 7-by-11-by-2-in [17-by-28-by-5-cm] baking pan.

In a small bowl, combine the flour, baking soda, and salt. Set aside.

In a large bowl, with a hand mixer, beat together the butter, granulated sugar, and brown sugar on high speed until light and fluffy, about 3 minutes. Beat in the egg and vanilla until smooth. Gradually beat in the flour mixture until combined. Stir in the walnuts and chocolate chips. Spread the dough evenly into the prepared pan.

Bake for 20 to 25 minutes, or until golden brown and a toothpick inserted into the center comes out clean. Let cool completely in the pan. When ready to serve, cut into 2-in [5-cm] squares. Store wrapped tightly in plastic wrap at room temperature for up to 1 week. To freeze, cut into four large sections and remove from the pan. Wrap the sections tightly in plastic wrap. Place the sections in a zip-top freezer bag and push out all the air. Freeze for up to 1 month. Let the wrapped sections defrost in the refrigerator overnight.

**MAKES TWENTY 2-IN [5-CM] BARS**

# CHEWY CHIP BARS

We used to make these bars for our road trips to Lake Tahoe. My brother and I would nibble on them in the back of our red Volvo station wagon as we made our way up and over the pass, with Dad's *Cruisin' Classics* tape on full blast. They're still my go-to recipe for road trips up to the mountains or even down the coast with my girl-friends. These bars are hearty, moist, and creamy with just the right texture, thanks to the oat and coconut combo, and they'll keep you satisfied until your next rest stop. To dress them up a little, slice the bars, wrap them in parchment paper, and tie the package with baker's twine.

1⅓ cups [160 g] all-purpose flour

½ tsp baking soda

½ tsp ground cinnamon

¼ tsp salt

½ cup [110 g] unsalted butter, at room temperature

1 cup [200 g] firmly packed dark brown sugar

1 large egg

1 tsp vanilla extract

3 Tbsp whole milk

¾ cup [125 g] dried cranberries

1 cup [90 g] unsweetened shredded coconut

¾ cup [60 g] old-fashioned rolled oats

1½ cups [255 g] Guittard Milk Chocolate Baking Chips

Preheat the oven to 350°F [180°C]. Lightly butter a 9-by-13-by-2-in [23-by-33-by-5-cm] baking pan.

In a small bowl, combine the flour, baking soda, cinnamon, and salt. Set aside.

In a large bowl, with a hand mixer, beat together the butter and brown sugar on high speed until light and smooth, about 3 minutes. Beat in the egg, vanilla, and milk until smooth. Gradually beat in the flour mixture until combined. Stir in the cranberries, coconut, oats, and chocolate chips until just combined. Spread the dough evenly in the prepared pan.

Bake for 35 to 40 minutes, or until a toothpick inserted into the center comes out clean. If the top begins to brown too quickly, cover the pan loosely with aluminum foil. Let cool completely in the pan. When ready to serve, cut into 3-in [7.5-cm] squares. Store in an airtight container at room temperature for up to 1 week. To freeze, cut into four large sections and remove from the pan. Wrap the sections tightly in plastic wrap. Place the sections in a zip-top freezer bag and push out all the air. Freeze for up to 1 month. Let the wrapped sections defrost in the refrigerator overnight.

**MAKES TWENTY 3-IN [7.5-CM] BARS**

*Chapter 4*

# CAKES, CUPCAKES, TARTS & PIE

# FLOURLESS CHOCOLATE CAKE

My grandfather loved the simple things in life: the San Francisco Seals (the Major League base- ball team before the Giants), spending time in the mountains with his sons, and making great chocolate. This was one of his favorite recipes— a simple and straight-to-the-point chocolate cake, because sometimes a simple recipe can be the best kind of recipe. This cake calls for only five ingredients, and no flour whatsoever, so the flavor of the chocolate really shines. It can be served plain or dressed up. Consider adding Whipped Cream (page 170) and seasonal berries, Chocolate Crème Fraîche Frosting (page 168), Lemon Buttercream (see Yo Yos, page 63), or a drizzling of Salted Caramel (page 167).

**3½ oz [100 g] Guittard Bittersweet Chocolate Baking Bars, broken into small pieces**

**½ cup [110 g] unsalted butter, at room temperature**

**¾ cup [150 g] superfine sugar**

**3 large eggs, lightly beaten**

**½ cup [50 g] Guittard Cocoa Rouge (Dutch-processed unsweetened cocoa powder)**

Preheat the oven to 375°F [190°C]. Line an 8-in [20-cm] square cake pan with parchment paper on the bottom, along the sides, and with 2 to 3 in [5 to 7.5 cm] paper hanging over the sides, and butter the paper.

Melt the chocolate and butter together using a hot water bath or the microwave oven (see Note: Melting Chocolate, page 51). Stir until completely melted and smooth. Remove the bowl from the water if you used a hot water bath and set aside to cool for about 5 minutes.

Whisk the sugar, eggs, and cocoa powder into the cooled melted chocolate mixture. Pour the batter into the prepared pan.

Bake for 25 minutes, or until the top is cracked and the middle is just set. Let cool in the pan for 10 minutes, then remove the cake from the pan by slowly lifting the parchment paper, and set the cake on a wire rack to cool completely. Care- fully peel the parchment paper from the cake and serve. To freeze, wrap the cake tightly in plastic wrap, place the cake in a zip-top freezer bag, and push out all of the air. Freeze for up to 1 month. Let the wrapped cake defrost in the refrigerator overnight.

**MAKES ONE 8-IN [20-CM] SINGLE-LAYER CAKE**

# CHOCOLATE CARAMEL PECAN BUNDT CAKE

There's something about the patterns that emerge on this delicate cake that make me feel like I've been transported to my grandmother's kitchen in the 1950s. This is an all-in-one cake—caramel topping, pecan filling, and delicious cake that cook all at once! Guests will be convinced that you slaved over this Bundt cake, but it's really an easy recipe. Once you pop it in the oven, your work is done. I make this as often for brunch as I do for a dinner party dessert.

**1 Tbsp unsalted butter, plus 1 cup [220 g], at room temperature**

**2 Tbsp light corn syrup**

**1 Tbsp water**

**½ cup [100 g] firmly packed dark brown sugar**

**⅔ cup [80 g] pecan halves**

**3½ cups [525 g] Guittard Semisweet Chocolate Baking Wafers**

**1⅓ cups [160 g] all-purpose flour**

**⅛ tsp salt**

**6 large eggs**

**1 cup [200 g] granulated sugar**

**2 tsp vanilla extract**

**1 cup [170 g] Guittard Milk Chocolate Baking Chips or Guittard Butterscotch Baking Chips (optional)**

Preheat the oven to 350°F [180°C]. Butter a 9-in [23-cm] Bundt pan if it is not nonstick.

In a small microwave-safe bowl, combine the 1 Tbsp butter, corn syrup, water, and brown sugar. Microwave in 30-second intervals, stirring after each interval, until the butter is melted and the sugar has dissolved. Whisk until the mixture is smooth, pour into the prepared Bundt pan, and sprinkle in the pecans. Set aside.

Melt the semisweet chocolate wafers and the remaining 1 cup [220 g] butter together using a hot water bath or the microwave oven (see Note: Melting Chocolate, page 51). Stir until completely melted and smooth. Remove the bowl from the water if you used a hot water bath and set aside to cool.

In a small bowl, combine the flour and salt. Set aside.

In a large bowl, with a hand mixer, beat together the eggs, granulated sugar, and vanilla on high speed until the mixture is light and has doubled in volume, about 5 minutes. Stir in the cooled melted chocolate mixture on low speed. Gradually beat in the flour mixture until combined. Stir in the milk chocolate chips (if using). Pour the batter into the Bundt pan over the pecans.

CONTINUED

Bake for 50 to 55 minutes, or until a toothpick inserted into the cake comes out clean. Remove the pan from the oven. Place a large inverted serving platter over the cake and quickly flip the cake upside down, gently shaking it to loosen the cake from the pan. Let the Bundt pan sit on top of the platter for up to 10 minutes to let all of the caramel drip out onto the plate. Cool completely before serving. Store in an airtight container at room temperature for up to 2 days.

**MAKES ONE 9-IN [23-CM] BUNDT CAKE**

# BLACK BOTTOM CUPCAKES

These cupcakes are moist and dense with a cheesecake filling that cooks along with the cake. The filling bubbles up through the center so you get cream cheese and dark chocolate with each bite. Plus they're sturdy and easy to schlep over the hills of San Francisco without worrying about smudged frosting. This recipe can be easily made into a cake, too (see Variation).

## BATTER

1½ cups [180 g] all-purpose flour

1 cup plus 1 Tbsp [215 g] sugar

⅓ cup [35 g] Guittard Cocoa Rouge (Dutch-processed unsweetened cocoa powder)

½ tsp baking soda

¼ tsp salt

1 cup [240 ml] cold water

¼ cup [60 ml] vegetable oil

1 Tbsp white vinegar

1½ tsp vanilla extract

## FILLING

½ cup [115 g] cream cheese, at room temperature

2 Tbsp sugar

2 tsp whole milk

½ cup [85 g] Guittard Semisweet Chocolate Baking Chips

Preheat the oven to 350°F [180°C]. Line twelve cupcake cups with paper liners.

**To make the batter:** In a large bowl, combine the flour, sugar, cocoa powder, baking soda, and salt. Make a well in the center of the flour mixture and pour the water, vegetable oil, vinegar, and vanilla into the well. Whisk until blended; the batter will still be lumpy.

CONTINUED

**To make the filling:** In a medium bowl, with a hand mixer, beat together the cream cheese and sugar until smooth. Add the milk and beat until combined. Stir in the chocolate chips.

Divide the batter among the twelve prepared cupcake cups. Add 1 Tbsp of the filling to the center of each cupcake.

Bake for 25 to 30 minutes, or until a toothpick inserted into the chocolate cake portion comes out clean. Remove the cupcakes from the pan and cool on a wire rack. Store in an airtight container at room temperature for up to 1 week.

**MAKES TWELVE CUPCAKES**

**Variation for Black Bottom Cake:** Butter a 9-by-5-by-3-in [23-by-12-by-7.5-cm] loaf pan. Pour the batter into the pan. Add the filling, 1 Tbsp at a time, down the middle of the pan, keeping it away from the edges. Leave the dots of filling in the middle of the cake, or use a knife to swirl the filling around. Bake for 45 minutes, or until a toothpick inserted into the cake portion comes out clean. Transfer to a wire rack to cool completely. Cut into 1-in [2.5-cm] slices and serve. Store in the loaf pan wrapped tightly with plastic wrap at room temperature for up to 1 week.

# CHOCOLATE BERRY TART

My aunt Vicki and uncle Peter live about an hour and a half north of San Francisco in a little town on the Russian River. Growing up, we'd spend our summer days floating down the river and the evenings picking blackberries from the bushes around their property. Even now, whenever we visit them, my brother Jesse, his wife, Alice, and I walk down the road with strainers in hand, armed and ready to see who can bring back the biggest berry haul. Blackberries and chocolate may not seem like a typical combination, but the two work deliciously together. Juicy berries top the sweet cream filling; the chocolate crust and ganache layer deliver an intense chocolate flavor. When I can't find good blackberries, I use raspberries, which look so pretty atop this tart, but you can use any other yummy berry at hand, such as fresh strawberries or olallieberries.

## TART SHELL

¾ cup [90 g] all-purpose flour

¼ cup [20 g] Guittard Cocoa Rouge (Dutch-processed unsweetened cocoa powder)

2 Tbsp cacao nibs

Pinch of salt

¼ cup [55 g] unsalted butter, at room temperature

¼ cup [50 g] granulated sugar

1 large egg

Chocolate Ganache (page 165)

## FILLING

1 cup [230 g] cream cheese, at room temperature

1 cup [200 g] superfine sugar

¼ cup [20 g] Guittard Cocoa Rouge (Dutch-processed unsweetened cocoa powder)

1½ cups [215 g] fresh raspberries or blackberries

CONTINUED

**To make the tart shell:** In a small bowl, combine the flour, cocoa powder, cacao nibs, and salt. Set aside.

In a large bowl, with a hand mixer, beat together the butter and granulated sugar until light and fluffy, about 3 minutes. Add the egg and beat until smooth. Gradually beat in the flour mixture until the dough comes together in a ball. Form the dough into a disk, wrap tightly with plastic wrap, and refrigerate for at least 1 hour, or up to 4 days. (The dough can also be frozen for up to 3 weeks. Defrost in the refrigerator overnight before using.)

Preheat the oven to 325°F [165°C]. Set aside a 4-by-13-in [10-by-33-cm] or 9-in [23-cm] tart pan.

On a lightly floured work surface, roll out the chilled dough to 5 by 14 in [12 by 35.5 cm] or a 10-in [25-cm] round, dusting with a little more flour as needed to keep it from sticking. If the dough gets too sticky, put it back in the refrigerator for about 15 minutes and add a little more flour to your work surface. Roll the round of dough onto the rolling pin and carefully unroll the dough into the tart pan. Press the dough down into the bottom of the pan and up the sides. Using a fork, poke holes in the dough to keep it from puffing up too much while baking.

Bake the crust for 6 to 8 minutes, or until the dough is puffed and slightly darker around the edges. The crust will still look a little doughy in the center, but it will set as it cools. Let cool completely on a wire rack.

When the crust is cool, pour the ganache into the shell and spread it out evenly. Set aside.

**To make the filling:** In a large bowl, with a hand mixer, beat together the cream cheese, superfine sugar, and cocoa powder until combined, thick, and fluffy, about 3 minutes.

Pour the filling into the crust and spread it evenly over the ganache. Place the berries on the top in any design you'd like. Refrigerate the tart for at least 1 hour, or overnight, then slice into wedges and serve. Store in an airtight container in the refrigerator for up to 2 days.

**MAKES ONE 4-BY-13-IN [10-BY-33-CM] OR 9-IN [23-CM] ROUND TART**

# CHOCOLATE MOUSSE PIE

San Francisco isn't known for ideal beach weather, but that didn't stop our family from spending time at the ocean. We'd head out to Baker Beach and my brother and I would spend a few hours running through the fog in our bathing suits. One of our favorite things to do on a beach day was make mud pies—those easy-to-make pies of water and sand that would bake up into an imaginary, delicious treat. This recipe is exactly what we were pretending to make but so much more delectable. It's also an easy make-ahead recipe because the crust, filling, and whipped cream can be made a day ahead of serving. Slice into generous servings and you'll be delighted with this dense and intense chocolate pie.

½ cup [110 g] unsalted butter

3 cups [200 g] chocolate wafer cookies

¼ cup [50 g] firmly packed dark brown sugar

Pinch of salt

Chocolate Mousse (page 111)

Whipped Cream (page 170)

2 Tbsp chocolate shavings

Preheat the oven to 375°F [190°C]. Butter a 9-in [23-cm] pie pan.

In a medium saucepan, melt the butter over medium heat. Set aside.

Using a food processor, process the wafer cookies until they are fine crumbs, about 45 seconds. Add the brown sugar, melted butter, and salt and process until the crumb mixture is the consistency of wet sand. Pour the mixture into the prepared pie pan and press the crumbs into the bottom of the pan and up the sides.

Bake for 7 to 10 minutes, or until the surface is firm. Remove the pie crust from the oven and let cool completely. (At this point, you can wrap the crust tightly in plastic wrap and refrigerate overnight.)

Pour the chocolate mousse into the pie crust and spread it evenly. Refrigerate the pie until the mousse is firm, 3 hours or overnight. (If you're letting the pie set overnight, be sure to cover it with plastic wrap.) Spread the whipped cream over the mousse. Sprinkle the chocolate shavings over the top. Serve immediately. Store in an airtight container in the refrigerator for up to 3 days.

**MAKES ONE 9-IN [23-CM] PIE**

# CHOCOLATE CHEESECAKE

Our chief operating officer, Gerry, loves sweets. He's always the first to dive into any new recipe I bring into the office. He'll take a few bites, consider, and then proceed to describe the taste and character of every bite as he savors the treat. This recipe is one of his favorites. Think of your favorite cheesecake recipe gone chocolate—the crust is a graham cracker base blended with cocoa powder, the filling is cheesecake with chocolate chips, and a hard bittersweet chocolate shell tops it off. Put them together and what do you get? Gerry's favorite chocolate cheesecake.

**CRUST**

10 graham crackers (10 rectangles)

2 Tbsp Guittard Cocoa Rouge (Dutch-processed unsweetened cocoa powder)

4 Tbsp [55 g] unsalted butter, melted and cooled

1 Tbsp cacao nibs

**FILLING**

3 cups [690 g] cream cheese, at room temperature

1 cup [200 g] sugar

3 Tbsp all-purpose flour

1 tsp vanilla extract

4 egg whites, at room temperature

1 cup [170 g] Guittard Semisweet Chocolate Baking Chips

**Chocolate Shell (page 166)**

**To make the crust:** Preheat the oven to 325°F [165°C].

Using a food processor, process the graham crackers until they are coarse crumbs, about 30 seconds. Add the cocoa powder and pulse five times, then add the butter and pulse until the mixture is the consistency of wet sand. Add the cacao nibs and pulse two times. Pour the crumb mixture into a 9-in [23-cm] springform pan and press the crumbs into the bottom of the pan.

Bake for 5 minutes, or until just toasted and firm. Let cool on a wire rack.

**To make the filling:** In a large bowl, with a hand mixer, beat the cream cheese until smooth. Add the sugar and flour and beat until fluffy, about 2 minutes.

In a liquid measuring cup, mix the vanilla and egg whites with a fork until just combined. Pour the egg mixture into the cream cheese mixture and blend until smooth. Stir in the chocolate chips.

Pour the filling into the cooled crust and bake for 35 minutes. Cool on a wire rack for 30 minutes, then refrigerate overnight. (At this point, you can wrap the cheesecake, still in the pan, in plastic wrap and freeze for up to 1 month. Let the cheese-cake defrost in the refrigerator overnight.)

Release and remove the sides of the springform pan. Pour the chocolate shell over the cheese-cake and place in the refrigerator to chill for 15 to 20 minutes, or until the shell is hard. Store in an airtight container in the refrigerator for up to 5 days.

**MAKES ONE 9-IN [23-CM] CHEESECAKE**

## Chapter 5

# PUDDINGS, BONBONS, FUDGE & CONFECTIONS

# CHOCOLATE PUDDING

This recipe is a traditional American chocolate pudding—creamy, rich, and completely nostalgic. In fact, it's so quintessentially American that one of my dad's favorite memories is eating it while watching *American Bandstand* after coming home from school. This simple recipe warrants using the best ingredients you can find, and being as patient as possible while waiting for the pudding to cool. Use the recipe as a filling, a layer in a trifle (see page 118), or just pour it into a wide-mouth canning jar, spoon some whipped cream on top, and voilà—a simple but outstanding dessert.

¾ cup [90 g] confectioners' sugar

3 Tbsp cornstarch

⅛ tsp salt

3 cups [720 ml] whole milk

6 oz [170 g] Guittard Bittersweet Chocolate Baking Bars, broken into pieces

1 tsp vanilla extract

Whipped Cream (page 170) for serving (optional)

Whisk together the confectioners' sugar, corn-starch, and salt in a medium saucepan. Slowly whisk in the milk over medium heat, until the milk is hot but not boiling. Add the chocolate, whisking occasionally, until the chocolate is melted. Increase the heat to medium-high and bring the mixture to a slow boil, while continuously whisking the bottom and sides for 10 to 15 minutes, or until the mixture thickens. Remove from the heat and whisk in the vanilla.

Pour the pudding into eight ½-cup [120-ml] ramekins or small bowls, or a large bowl (if planning to use for a trifle). Let sit at room temperature for 10 minutes. Place plastic wrap directly on the surface of the pudding to prevent a skin from forming, and refrigerate for at least 4 hours, or overnight. The pudding will thicken as it cools. Serve chilled, with whipped cream, if desired. Store covered in plastic wrap in the refrigerator for up to 4 days.

**MAKES EIGHT ½-CUP [120-ML] SERVINGS**

# CHOCOLATE MOUSSE

This recipe is a bit of a time warp, taking you back to a dessert classic—a chocolate mousse so thick that you could turn the bowl over and it wouldn't go anywhere. It's rich and creamy and super chocolatey. And you can pair it with something light and sweet like Whipped Cream (page 170), sliced fresh strawberries, or Sinful Chocolate Pound Cake (page 146) or use it as the filling in our Chocolate Mousse Pie (page 105).

**1¾ cups [270 g] Guittard Semisweet Chocolate Baking Wafers**

**1 cup [240 ml] heavy whipping cream, chilled**

**2 Tbsp liqueur, such as Kahlúa, Grand Marnier, or Framboise**

**3 egg whites, at room temperature**

**¼ cup [50 g] superfine sugar**

Melt the chocolate wafers using a hot water bath or the microwave oven (see Note: Melting Chocolate, page 51). Stir until completely melted and smooth. Remove the bowl from the water if you used a hot water bath and set aside to cool.

In a cold medium bowl, using a hand mixer with chilled beaters, beat the cream until soft peaks form. Beat in the liqueur to combine. Set aside.

In the clean, dry bowl of a stand mixer with the whisk attachment (or in a large bowl using a hand mixer fitted with whisk beaters), beat the egg whites on low speed until frothy, then increase the speed to medium-high and gradually add the sugar, beating until stiff peaks form.

With a rubber spatula, gently fold the cooled chocolate into the egg white mixture. Fold in the whipped cream until just combined. Pour the mousse into eight ½-cup [120-ml] ramekins or small bowls and refrigerate for 3 hours. Serve chilled. Store covered with plastic wrap in the refrigerator for up to 2 days.

**MAKES EIGHT ½-CUP [120-ML] SERVINGS**

# CHOCOLATE POTS DE CRÈME

My dad's cousin Mimi loves this treat. Her mother, Camille, one of San Francisco's original "foodies," was always entertaining, often hosting James Beard as the guest of honor. During these dinner parties, young Mimi would sit at the top of the staircase happily munching on portions of the multicourse dinner while watching the parties unfold. Mimi's favorite course was always dessert, and pots de crème were something Camille excelled at making. Pots de crème are one of those desserts that—while not all that difficult to make—tells guests that they merit something special.

## POTS DE CRÈME

6 oz [170 g] Guittard Semisweet Chocolate Baking Bars, broken into small pieces

¼ cup [60 ml] whole milk

2¼ cups [600 ml] heavy whipping cream

¼ vanilla bean pod (see Note)

2 Tbsp superfine sugar

4 egg yolks, at room temperature

1 tsp vanilla extract

## ESPRESSO GRANITA

1 shot espresso, cooled

1 cup [240 ml] warm water

⅓ cup [65 g] granulated sugar

1 tsp coffee-flavored liqueur, such as Kahlúa

Whipped Cream (page 170) for serving (optional)

**To make the pots de crème:** Preheat the oven to 325°F [165°C]. Place the chocolate in a medium heatproof bowl. Set aside.

In a medium saucepan, combine the milk and cream. Add the vanilla bean seeds and pod (see Note: Using Vanilla Beans, page 114) and bring to a boil, stirring frequently. Pour the hot milk mixture over the chocolate and let steep for 3 to 5 minutes. Whisk the liquid until the chocolate is melted and the mixture is smooth.

CONTINUED

In a large bowl, whisk together the superfine sugar, egg yolks, and vanilla extract until you've created a paste. Add the chocolate mixture to the sugar mixture and whisk until the batter is smooth, about 2 minutes.

Set a strainer or sieve over a large bowl and pour the chocolate mixture into the strainer. Strain the mixture using a rubber spatula to move the mixture around and lightly press it through. Don't push too hard; you want to avoid letting through any lumps or the vanilla bean pod. Discard the pod and any debris in the strainer.

Pour ½ cup [120 ml] of the strained chocolate mixture into eight ½-cup [120-ml] ramekins. Set the ramekins in a deep baking pan and carefully pour hot water into the pan, to about halfway up the sides of the ramekins. Cover the baking pan loosely with foil.

Bake for 40 minutes. Let the ramekins cool on a wire rack for 10 minutes, then transfer them to the refrigerator to chill for 1 hour. (At this point, you can wrap each ramekin tightly with plastic wrap and store in the refrigerator for up to 3 days.)

**To make the espresso granita:** In a small bowl, whisk together the espresso, warm water, granulated sugar, and liqueur until the sugar dissolves. Line an 8- to 9-in [20- to 23-cm] cake pan with plastic wrap and pour the espresso mixture into the pan. Place the pan in the freezer. Every 30 minutes, scrape the mixture with a fork (without tearing the plastic wrap) until the granita resembles finely shaved ice. This should take four to five scrapings over 2 to 3 hours.

Take the ramekins out of the refrigerator. Scoop a spoonful of whipped cream (if using) and 2 to 3 tsp of the granita onto each of the pots de crème. Serve immediately.

**MAKES EIGHT ½-CUP [120-ML] SERVINGS**

**NOTE:** USING VANILLA BEANS. With a sharp knife, carefully cut the vanilla bean pod (the amount of bean pod called for in the recipe) down the center lengthwise, being careful not to cut it all the way through. Open the pod like a book to expose all of the small seeds inside. Using your knife, gently scrape as many of the seeds as you can into the liquid used in the recipe, such as milk in a small saucepan, then drop the pod into the milk. Mix to incorporate and bring the milk to a boil. The seeds, oil, and pod will infuse the liquid with intense vanilla flavor. Then proceed with the recipe. Discard the vanilla pod after use, or rinse and dry it off and bury it in your sugar canister to flavor your sugar.

# CHOCOLATE-COCONUT PANNA COTTA

While my dad's side of the family is French and Irish, my mom's side is Italian. In honor of my Italian side, the Avenali family, it's only fitting that I include this lovely, refreshing dessert. *Panna cotta*—"cooked milk"—is an Italian classic: sophisticated and rich, with a silky texture. I make my version with coconut milk, which adds a tropical nuttiness, but you can make it with whipping cream if you prefer the traditional dairy flavor.

**1½ cups [360 ml] coconut milk or heavy whipping cream**

**2½ tsp unflavored powdered gelatin**

**2 Tbsp superfine sugar**

**⅔ cup [100 g] Guittard Milk Chocolate Baking Wafers**

**1 tsp vanilla extract**

**Seasonal fruit for serving**

Pour the coconut milk into a medium saucepan and sprinkle the gelatin over the top. Let the gelatin absorb the milk for 10 minutes. Add the superfine sugar and chocolate wafers and whisk over medium-low heat until the gelatin and chocolate have dissolved. Remove from the heat and stir in the vanilla.

Set a strainer over a large bowl and pour the chocolate mixture into the strainer. Use a rubber spatula to move the mixture around and lightly press the mixture through the strainer. Don't push too hard; you want to avoid letting through any lumps. Pour the strained mixture into six ⅓-cup [80-ml] molds, ramekins, or small, heatproof dessert bowls. Cover tightly with plastic wrap and refrigerate for at least 2 hours, or up to overnight. To unmold, set the molds in a bowl of warm water for 1 minute, then invert onto serving plates, tapping the mold until the panna cotta releases. Serve chilled with fresh or puréed seasonal fruit. Store covered with plastic wrap in the refrigerator for up to 5 days.

**MAKES SIX ⅓-CUP [80-ML] SERVINGS**

CONTINUED

**Variation for Panna Cotta Tricolore:** For an elegant dessert, make three batches of the panna cotta, one at a time, starting with the milk chocolate panna cotta, then the white chocolate, then the bittersweet chocolate. Divide the milk chocolate layer among six tall, glass dessert dishes, wrap with plastic wrap, and refrigerate for at least 1 hour, or up to 4 hours. While the first layer is setting, make the second layer, the white chocolate panna cotta. Remove the dishes from the refrigerator and set aside the plastic wrap. Pour the white chocolate layer into the dessert dishes, rewrap with the plastic wrap, and refrigerate for at least 1 hour, or up to 4 hours. Repeat with the bittersweet chocolate layer and refrigerate for at least 2 hours, or up to overnight. Serve chilled, topped with fresh or puréed seasonal fruit. Store covered with plastic wrap in the refrigerator for up to 4 days.

# CHOCOLATE TRIFLE

My grandmother loved to entertain, especially during the summer. She had favorite meals and favorite desserts for serving to her guests. After a day of lounging in the sun, the ladies would dress up for a candlelit, multicourse dinner. Most of the dinner parties I throw are more casual. While I use a party as a perfect excuse to pull out my pretty patterned linen napkins and to purchase enough bouquets to turn my apartment into a mini floral boutique, most of my dinner gatherings involve sitting on the floor eating family-style fare. But even the most casual dinner party warrants a dessert that's sophisticated—like this trifle, a fixture at my grandmother's summertime soirées. I like serving this treat in vintage glasses as a tribute to my granny. You have room for creativity with this dessert. The bottom layer can be crumbled cookies, diced-up brownies, or even pound cake. (Don't use fresh brownies or cookies; be sure they are at least a day old to avoid moisture accumulating in the serving dish.) The middle layer is whipped cream, which can be flavored or just slightly sweetened, and the top layer is chocolate pudding. Simply divine. For a more traditional presentation, layer the ingredients in one large glass bowl.

**4 day-old Cocoa Brownies (page 85) or Chewy Chocolate Chip Cookies (page 48)**

**1 cup [240 ml] Whipped Cream (page 170)**

**1 cup [240 ml] Chocolate Pudding (page 110)**

**¼ cup [10 g] chocolate shavings**

Cut the brownies into small cubes, or break the cookies into small pieces, and divide among four short glasses, dessert cups, ramekins, or pretty coffee mugs. Spread about ¼ cup [60 ml] of the whipped cream into each glass, then add ¼ cup [60 ml] of the pudding. Sprinkle with the chocolate shavings and serve. Store wrapped tightly with plastic wrap in the refrigerator for up to 1 day.

**MAKES 4 SERVINGS**

# CHOCOLATE SOUFFLÉS

My dad, Gary, is a discerning sweets eater. He definitely has a few favorites, like this soufflé. Rich and intense, it has a robust chocolate flavor and an enticingly delicate texture that's sure to satisfy the most sophisticated palates. Baking soufflés in small ramekins means less worry about whether they will rise perfectly. Better yet, the individual servings ensure that you get your fair share without having to worry that a sweets lover like my dad might steal the last bite. If you don't have ramekins, bake your soufflés in ovenproof ceramic mugs that are about the same size.

**5 oz [140 g] Guittard Semisweet Chocolate Baking Bars, broken into small pieces**

**1 Tbsp whole milk**

**2 large eggs, separated, plus 1 egg white, at room temperature**

**⅛ tsp cream of tartar**

**½ cup plus 2 Tbsp [130 g] sugar**

Preheat the oven to 375°F [190°C]. Butter the insides of six ½-cup [120-ml] ramekins. Dust with sugar to coat. Shake out any excess sugar. Divide one-third of the chocolate pieces among the ramekins.

Melt the remaining chocolate and milk together using a hot water bath or the microwave oven (see Note: Melting Chocolate, page 51). Stir until completely melted and smooth. Remove the bowl from the water if you used a hot water bath and set aside to cool for 5 minutes. Whisk in the egg yolks. Set aside.

In the clean, dry bowl of a stand mixer fitted with the whisk attachment (or in a large bowl using a hand mixer fitted with whisk beaters), beat the egg whites and cream of tartar on medium-high speed until foamy. Gradually add the sugar and continue beating until soft peaks form. Gently whisk one-third of the egg white mixture into the chocolate mixture to lighten it, then gently whisk the chocolate mixture into the remaining egg white mixture until just combined, being careful not to overmix so the egg white mixture won't deflate. Divide the soufflé batter evenly among the prepared ramekins, filling to cover the chocolate pieces.

Bake for 12 to 15 minutes, or until the tops are puffed and crusty. Serve immediately.

**MAKES SIX ½-CUP [120-ML] CHOCOLATE SOUFFLÉS**

# DARK CHOCOLATE RASPBERRY BONBONS

One summer while working in the research and development kitchen, I was given a task: Come up with a recipe for the Collection Etienne line of chocolates, which we'd just introduced. I love combining fruit and chocolate, and this recipe is rather easy once you master the ganache (see Note: Rescuing Ganache, page 165). I like the texture that extra-seedy raspberry jam adds to these bonbons, but you can use a seedless jam if you prefer.

6 oz [170 g] Guittard Semisweet Chocolate Baking Bars, broken into small pieces

¼ cup [60 ml] heavy whipping cream

1 Tbsp raspberry preserves

½ cup [55 g] finely chopped pecans, walnuts, or almonds (optional)

3 Tbsp Guittard Cocoa Rouge (Dutch-processed unsweetened cocoa powder)

Melt the chocolate and cream together using a hot water bath or the microwave oven (see Note: Melting Chocolate, page 51). Stir until completely melted and smooth. Remove the bowl from the water if you used a hot water bath and set aside to cool.

Stir the raspberry preserves and nuts (if using) into the melted chocolate. Let the chocolate mixture cool for 15 minutes. Cover the bowl with plastic wrap and chill for 3 hours, or until the chocolate mixture is firm enough to handle.

Line a baking sheet with wax paper or parchment paper. Set aside. Pour the cocoa powder into a small, shallow dish.

Using a scoop or teaspoon, form the chilled chocolate mixture into 1-in [2.5-cm] balls. Roll the chocolate balls between the palms of your hands to smooth them out, without handling them too much. Roll each ball in the cocoa powder to coat and place on the prepared baking sheet. Refrigerate the bonbons for 1 to 5 hours, then serve chilled. Store in an airtight container in the refrigerator for up to 2 weeks.

**MAKES SIXTEEN 1-IN [2.5-CM] BONBONS**

# BOOZY BONBONS

Boxes of bonbons appear around the Guittard office regularly, but they don't last very long. Even people who taste chocolate every day find a good bonbon difficult to resist. These bonbons are simple with clear, irresistible flavors and can be a refined and stylish way to get your post-meal chocolate fix. The recipe calls for Grand Marnier, but feel free to use any liqueur that suits your fancy. Just be forewarned: Coating a bitter-sweet ganache ball in cocoa powder means not caring whether you get cocoa powder on your lips and shirt.

**6 oz [170 g] Guittard Bittersweet Chocolate Baking Bars, broken into small pieces**

**2 Tbsp unsalted butter**

**2 Tbsp heavy whipping cream**

**1 Tbsp Grand Marnier**

**3 Tbsp Guittard Cocoa Rouge (Dutch-processed unsweetened cocoa powder)**

Melt the chocolate, butter, and cream together using a hot water bath or the microwave oven (see Note: Melting Chocolate, page 51). Stir until completely melted and smooth. Stir in the Grand Marnier. Remove the bowl from the water if you used a hot water bath and set aside to cool for 15 minutes.

Cover the bowl with plastic wrap and chill for 3 hours, or until the chocolate mixture is firm enough to handle.

Line a baking sheet with wax paper or parchment paper. Set aside. Put the cocoa powder into a small, shallow dish.

Using a scoop or teaspoon, form the chilled chocolate mixture into 1-in [2.5-cm] balls. Roll the chocolate balls between the palms of your hands to smooth them out, making sure not to handle them too much. Roll each ball in the cocoa powder to coat and place on the prepared baking sheet. Refrigerate the bonbons for 1 to 5 hours, then serve chilled. Store in an airtight container in the refrigerator for up to 2 weeks.

**MAKES SIXTEEN 1-IN [2.5-CM] BONBONS**

# CHOCOLATE ALMOND GINGER BARK

I'm my father's daughter in many ways, one of which is our love for chocolate-covered ginger. This bark takes me back to the days when I lived in New York City. On occasion, I'd pop into Chef Andrew Shotts's studio and help box his gorgeous confections. It was always a treat when I came on a day when he was working with ginger, because I knew he would send some home with me.

Chocolate bark is an easy-to-make confection and completely versatile. This recipe uses almonds and bits of candied ginger, but you can always try different combinations and play with colors and textures. Because this chocolate bark is beautiful with a distinctive flavor, it makes a perfect gift for almost any occasion. I often make it as a holiday present or bring it as a house-warming gift.

**2 cups [230 g] sliced almonds**

**¼ cup [30 g] confectioners' sugar**

**2 Tbsp light corn syrup**

**1 Tbsp warm water**

**½ cup [50 g] candied ginger or other dried or candied fruits, cut into ¼-in [2.5-cm] dice**

**2¼ cups [340 g] Guittard Bittersweet or Semisweet Chocolate Baking Wafers**

Preheat the oven to 350°F [180°C]. Line a rimmed baking sheet with parchment paper.

In a small bowl, combine the almonds, confectioners' sugar, corn syrup, and water and mix until the sugar has dissolved. Pour the almond mixture onto the prepared baking sheet, and spread it in a thin, even layer covering the entire sheet.

Toast the almond mixture for about 15 minutes, stirring occasionally, until the almonds are golden brown. Remove from the oven and let the mixture cool in the pan on a wire rack.

When the almond mixture has cooled to room temperature, add it to a medium bowl along with the candied ginger and mix to combine. Set aside.

CONTINUED

Melt the chocolate using a hot water bath or the microwave oven (see Note: Melting Chocolate, page 51). Stir until completely melted and smooth. Remove the bowl from the water if you used a hot water bath and cool the chocolate to 95°F [35°C].

Add the melted chocolate to the bowl with the almond-ginger mixture and stir until the almonds and ginger pieces are uniformly coated. Pour the mixture onto the prepared baking sheet (re-line with parchment paper, if necessary), and use an offset spatula to spread it out evenly, working quickly so the chocolate does not set before an even layer can be created. Let cool at room temperature for 30 minutes, then refrigerate until the chocolate is hard, at least 3 hours and up to overnight.

Break the chocolate bark into pieces. Store in an airtight container in a cool place for up to 2 weeks.

**MAKES TWENTY 2-IN [5-CM] CHUNKS**

# ROCKY MOUNTAINS

Back in the '60s, my parents lived in Colorado, where my dad would rock climb during the summer and ski during the winter. These little coconut-marshmallow mountains make me think of him whenever I make them—the homemade version of a rocky road candy. They're delicious, make a great gift, and forming them is just a matter of melting two different kinds of chocolate.

**2¼ cups [340 g] Guittard Milk Chocolate Baking Wafers**

**3 tsp vegetable oil**

**1 cup [110 g] chopped almonds, walnuts, or pecans**

**1 cup [70 g] miniature marshmallows**

**1 cup [170 g] Guittard Choc-Au-Lait Baking Chips (white chocolate)**

**2 Tbsp unsweetened shredded coconut**

Line a baking sheet with parchment paper.

Melt the milk chocolate and 2 tsp of the vegetable oil together using a hot water bath or the microwave oven (see Note: Melting Chocolate, page 51). Stir until completely melted and smooth. Remove the bowl from the water if you used a hot water bath and cool the chocolate to 95°F [35°C]. (Keep the water in the saucepan; you will use it again.) Add the almonds and marshmallows and stir until the mixture is smooth.

Drop the chocolate mixture by rounded teaspoonful onto the prepared baking sheet. Form each candy into a peak shape by lightly pressing from the bottom up the sides. Refrigerate for 10 to 15 minutes until set.

Melt the white chocolate chips and remaining 1 tsp oil together in the hot water bath (or microwave), stirring occasionally until the chocolate is smooth. Set aside and let cool for 5 minutes; it will melt the candies if it's too hot.

Remove the candies from the refrigerator and spoon the cooled melted white chocolate mixture over each mountain, allowing it to drip down like snow. Lightly press some of the shredded coconut on top of each candy. Refrigerate for an additional 5 minutes until set. Store in an airtight container in the refrigerator for up to 1 week.

**MAKES FIFTEEN LARGE OR THIRTY SMALL CANDIES**

# JIM'S SPECIAL FUDGE

Jim worked for us as a cacao bean buyer for more than twenty years. He loved fudge and used to bring his super-rich version to the factory on special occasions. After some begging (after a lot of begging!) he finally agreed to share the secret recipe. Jim's fudge is now an essential part of our potluck parties.

This recipe calls for only three ingredients, plus nuts, which are optional, making this fudge ideal for experimentation. You can add other ingredients if you like, topping with fleur de sel or cacao nibs. Try making fudge with a center ribbon of salted caramel, peanut butter, or marshmallow cream.

**2¾ cups [415 g] Guittard Semisweet Chocolate Baking Wafers**

**1¾ cups [420 ml] canned sweetened condensed milk**

**4 Tbsp unsalted butter**

**¾ cup [85 g] chopped walnuts, pecans, or almonds (optional)**

Line an 8-by-8-by-2-in [20-by-20-by-5-cm] baking pan with parchment paper along the bottom, up the sides, and overhanging the sides by about 1 in [2.5 cm].

Melt the chocolate, condensed milk, and butter together using a hot water bath or the microwave oven (see Note: Melting Chocolate, page 51). Stir until completely melted and smooth. Remove the bowl from the water if you used a hot water bath and mix in the nuts (if using). Pour the batter into the prepared pan, spread evenly, and let cool for 2 hours, or until firm.

Use the parchment paper to carefully lift the fudge out of the pan. Place the fudge on a cutting board, discard the parchment, and cut it into 1½-in [4-cm] squares. Store in an airtight container in the refrigerator for up to 10 days.

**MAKES TWENTY-FIVE 1½-IN [4-CM] SQUARES**

**Variation for Layered Fudge:** Pour half of the batter into the prepared pan and spread it evenly. Spread a second layer of ½ cup [125 g] peanut butter, ½ cup [115 g] Salted Caramel (page 167), or ½ cup [35 g] marshmallow cream. Then pour in the rest of the batter and spread it evenly. Let the fudge cool for 2 hours. When you're ready to serve, cut it into 1½-in [4-cm] squares. Store, wrapped tightly, in the refrigerator for up to 10 days.

# CHOCOLATE-DIPPED, GRAHAM CRACKER–ROLLED MALLOWS

Yup, that's the name of these confections because that's exactly what they are—devised and named by my mom, Lyn. (She claims she's not crafty, but the evidence speaks for itself.) Gooey and crunchy with a thin chocolate shell, these have become one of our favorite holiday treats. Everybody in my family looks forward to seeing her arrive with these packed in her festive red-topped Tupperware container. We wait 364 days for them because Mom only makes them for Christmas. Take it from someone with years of waiting experience: Don't limit yourself to making these just once a year.

**4 graham crackers (4 rectangles)**

**1¾ cups [270 g] Guittard Bittersweet Chocolate Baking Wafers**

**1 Tbsp sunflower oil or coconut oil**

**24 jumbo marshmallows**

Line a baking sheet with wax paper or parchment paper.

Using a food processor, process the graham crackers into small crumbs. Put the crumbs into a small, shallow bowl.

Melt the chocolate and sunflower oil together using a hot water bath or the microwave oven (see Note: Melting Chocolate, page 51). Stir until completely melted and smooth. Remove the bowl from the water if you used a hot water bath and set aside to cool for 30 minutes.

Using a skewer or fork, dip a marshmallow into the chocolate mixture and then roll it in the graham cracker crumbs. Place it on the prepared baking sheet. Repeat until you have dipped and rolled all the marshmallows.

Place the candies into the refrigerator so the chocolate can harden, about 30 minutes. Store in an airtight container in the refrigerator for up to 1 week.

**MAKES TWENTY-FOUR CANDIES**

# CHOCOLATE SORBET

Mark Twain once said, "The coldest winter I ever spent was a summer in San Francisco." It's true. When most folks are donning their summer dresses, we're hunkered down in our layers—facing the onshore winds and a fog so thick you can't see across the street. But come October, we finally get our summer; warranting corner lemonade stands, sleeping with the windows open, and cold desserts—like this chocolate sorbet. While sorbet is often assumed to be a lighter option, this is anything but. The combination of semi-sweet chocolate and cocoa powder infuses every spoonful with a refreshing yet intensely rich chocolate flavor. If you don't have an ice-cream maker, pop it in the freezer for 24 hours. It won't be as smooth but will be just as rich and delicious.

2¼ cups [540 ml] water

1 cup [200 g] sugar

⅔ cup [70 g] Guittard Cocoa Rouge (Dutch-processed unsweetened cocoa powder)

½ tsp salt

4½ oz [130 g] Guittard Semisweet Chocolate Baking Bars, broken into small pieces

½ tsp vanilla extract

In a large saucepan (yes, you must use a large pan or the mixture will bubble over—trust me), add 1½ cups [360 ml] of the water and whisk in the sugar, cocoa powder, and salt. Bring to a boil and let boil for 45 seconds, whisking continuously.

Remove the mixture from the heat. Stir in the chocolate until it's melted, then stir in the vanilla and the remaining ¾ cup [180 ml] water. Transfer the chocolate mixture to a blender and blend for 15 seconds. Chill the mixture thoroughly in the refrigerator, 30 to 45 minutes, then freeze it in your ice-cream maker according to the manufacturer's instructions. If you don't have an ice-cream maker, put the sorbet in a large bowl in the freezer, and stir every hour for the first 3 hours, then let it sit for 24 hours, until frozen, before serving. Store in an airtight container in the freezer for up to 2 months.

**MAKES 3 CUPS [720 ML]**

# Chapter 6
# CHEF'S CHAPTER

---

Most of the recipes in this book are family recipes, made by home cooks, often over generations. This chapter is a little different. Here, we feature recipes by Guittard's resident executive pastry chef, Donald Wressell. Donald has been a pastry chef for twenty years, and has baked for the Four Seasons in Beverly Hills. He has a deft touch with chocolate, and brings a chef's sensibilities to these desserts. The recipes in this chapter may be slightly more difficult than the other recipes in the book, but every single one of Donald's recipes is worth the effort—especially his Grandma's Chocolate Cake on page 150. He explains his recipes clearly, so even a beginning baker can make these with good results. His advice? Make all of these recipes by weight if you have a scale.

# CHOCOLATE DIAMANTS

This simple, classic butter cookie is an elegant addition to tea or after-dinner coffee. *Diamant* refers to the way the sugar on the cookies' rims glints in the light. Because the dough freezes well, you can double the recipe and freeze half. With the dough logs wrapped in parchment paper and then sealed in plastic wrap, they will keep for up to 3 months in the freezer. So whenever you'd like to serve cookies, defrost a log for 30 minutes at room temperature, and then slice and bake as many dough rounds as you need.

**DOUGH**

1 cup [220 g] unsalted butter, at room temperature

½ cup [100 g] sugar

¼ tsp salt

2 cups [240 g] all-purpose flour

½ cup [50 g] Guittard Cocoa Rouge (Dutch-processed unsweetened cocoa powder)

¼ tsp ground cinnamon, preferably Saigon cinnamon

**EGG WASH**

1 egg white, at room temperature

Pinch of salt

**NIB SUGAR**

2 Tbsp cacao nibs

2 Tbsp sugar

**To make the dough:** In the bowl of a stand mixer fitted with the paddle attachment (or in a large bowl using a hand mixer), beat together the butter, sugar, and salt until light and fluffy, about 3 minutes.

In a small bowl, sift together the flour, cocoa powder, and cinnamon. Add the flour mixture to the butter mixture, and mix until the dough just comes together. Move the dough to a clean work surface, break it into two parts, and roll each part into a log. Wrap the logs in plastic wrap and refrigerate for at least 1 hour, or up to overnight.

Preheat the oven to 340°F [170°C]. Line two baking sheets with parchment paper.

**To make the egg wash:** In a small bowl, whisk together the egg white and salt until small bubbles form. Set aside.

**To make the nib sugar:** Using a food processor, pulse the cacao nibs and sugar into fine particles, 30 to 45 seconds. Pour the nib sugar onto a flat plate or cutting board.

Remove the dough from the refrigerator and discard the plastic wrap. With a pastry brush, lightly glaze a log with a thin layer of the egg wash, and roll the log in the nib sugar. Repeat with the second log. Cut each log into ½-in [12-mm] slices and place the slices on the prepared baking sheets, leaving 1 in [2.5 cm] between the cookies.

Bake for 14 minutes, or until the tops are slightly puffed and cracked. Transfer the cookies to a wire rack to cool completely. Store in an airtight container at room temperature for up to 1 week.

**MAKES THIRTY 2-IN (5-CM) COOKIES**

# TRIPLE CHOCOLATE COOKIES

A rich explosion of chocolate with a brownie-like center, these flavor-packed cookies were an instant hit the first time Donald served them. Our vice president of industrial sales, Mark, can be coaxed into any meeting if he knows we'll have these waiting.

The batter, while easy to make, is sticky and a bit messy. You can either chill the dough in a buttered bowl for 30 to 60 minutes and then scoop spoonfuls onto a baking sheet before baking, or you can roll the batter into logs after lightly dusting your hands with cocoa powder and then wrap in parchment paper and chill. Serve these warm from the oven and you will warm the hearts of the most demanding chocolate lovers.

1¾ cups [255 g] Guittard Semisweet Chocolate Baking Wafers

9 Tbsp [130 g] unsalted butter, at room temperature

½ cup [120 ml] chocolate liqueur

½ cup [60 g] all-purpose flour

¼ tsp baking powder

½ tsp salt

3 large eggs

1⅓ cups [265 g] sugar

1 tsp vanilla extract

1 cup [170 g] Guittard Semisweet Chocolate Baking Chips or Guittard Milk Chocolate Baking Chips

Melt the semisweet chocolate wafers, butter, and chocolate liqueur together using a hot water bath or the microwave oven (see Note: Melting Chocolate, page 51). Stir until completely melted and smooth. Pour into a large bowl and set aside.

In a small bowl, sift together the flour, baking powder, and salt. Set aside.

In the bowl of a stand mixer fitted with the whisk attachment (or in a medium bowl using a hand mixer fitted with the whisk beaters), beat together the eggs and sugar on high speed for 3 to 5 minutes, until light ribbons form when you lift the whisk out. Add the vanilla and stir to combine.

Fold the egg mixture into the melted chocolate until just combined. Then fold in the flour mixture until incorporated. Fold in the chocolate chips. Cover with plastic wrap, placing the wrap directly on the dough to prevent a film from forming. Refrigerate the dough for at least 1 hour, or up to overnight. (At this point, you can roll the chilled dough into 2-in [5-cm] logs and wrap tightly in plastic wrap and freeze for up to 2 months. When you are ready to bake the cookies, defrost the dough in the refrigerator for 3 hours, then slice ½ in [12 mm] thick and bake as directed.)

Preheat the oven to 325°F [165°C]. Line two baking sheets with parchment paper.

Drop teaspoonfuls of dough onto the prepared baking sheets, leaving 2 in [5 cm] between the cookies; the cookies will spread as they bake.

Bake for 10 minutes, or until the tops are slightly cracked and the centers are soft. Cool on the baking sheets for 5 minutes before transferring the cookies to a wire rack to cool completely. Store in an airtight container at room temperature for up to 1 week.

**MAKES FORTY 3-IN [7.5-CM] COOKIES**

# ROASTED BANANA MARMALADE CHOCOLATE TART

The filling of this tart is a classic chocolate ganache to which you add one egg. The egg sets the chocolate but the texture is so luscious—dense, velvety, and yet sophisticated—you'll find that you turn to this recipe whenever you need to bring a dessert to any kind of gathering.

You fully bake the sweet dough shell and let it cool before pouring in the filling, and then bake the tart in a low oven—just 200°F [95°C]. You can watch as the transformation takes place: The filling lifts just slightly as it bakes. I think of this tart as elevated ganache set on a perfect platform.

## MILK CHOCOLATE CHANTILLY

1½ cups [225 g] Guittard Milk Chocolate Baking Wafers

3 cups [720 ml] heavy whipping cream

1 Tbsp light corn syrup

1 Tbsp honey

½ cup [75 g] malted milk powder

## TART SHELL

¾ cup [90 g] almond flour

1 cup [120 g] pastry flour

½ cup [50 g] Guittard Cocoa Rouge (Dutch-processed unsweetened cocoa powder)

Pinch of salt

1 cup [220 g] unsalted butter, at room temperature

⅔ cup [130 g] granulated sugar

5 egg yolks

## ROASTED BANANA MARMALADE

2 ripe bananas

2 Tbsp unsalted butter, cut into small cubes

1 vanilla bean (see Note: Using Vanilla Beans, page 114)

Juice from 1 orange

⅓ cup [70 g] raw or turbinado sugar

## FILLING

1⅓ cups [200 g] Guittard Bittersweet Chocolate Baking Wafers

3 Tbsp plus 2 tsp whole milk

⅔ cup [80 ml] heavy whipping cream

2 Tbsp unsalted butter, at room temperature

1 large egg

CONTINUED

**To make the milk chocolate chantilly:** Place the milk chocolate in a large heatproof bowl. Set aside.

In a medium saucepan, combine 1 cup [240 ml] of the cream, the corn syrup, honey, and malted milk powder and bring to a boil, stirring frequently. Pour the hot cream mixture over the milk chocolate, and let sit for 5 minutes. Then whisk the chocolate mixture until smooth. Add the remaining 2 cups [480 ml] cream and whisk until just combined. Place plastic wrap directly on the surface of the chocolate mixture and refrigerate for at least 30 minutes, or up to overnight.

**To make the tart shell:** In a small bowl, sift together the almond flour, pastry flour, cocoa powder, and salt. Set aside.

In a large bowl using a hand mixer, beat together the butter and granulated sugar until light and fluffy, about 3 minutes. Add the egg yolks and beat until smooth. Gradually add the flour mixture and beat until just combined.

Form the dough into a disk and wrap tightly with plastic wrap. Chill the dough in the refrigerator for at least 1 hour, or up to 4 days.

Preheat the oven to 325°F [165°C]. Set aside a 9-in [23-cm] tart pan.

On a lightly floured work surface, roll out the chilled dough to a 10-in [25-cm] round, dusting with more flour as needed to keep it from sticking. If the dough gets too sticky, put it back in the refrigerator for 15 minutes and add more flour to your work surface. Roll the round of dough onto the rolling pin and carefully unroll the dough onto the tart pan. Press the dough down into the bottom of the pan and up the sides. Using a fork, poke holes into the dough to keep it from puffing up too much while baking.

Bake for 6 to 8 minutes, or until the dough is puffed and slightly set around the edges. It will still look a little doughy in the center, but it will set as it cools. Let cool completely on a wire rack.

**To make the roasted banana marmalade:** Raise the oven temperature to 400°F [200°C].

Peel and cut the bananas into chunks and place the banana pieces and butter in an 8-by-11-in [20-by-28-cm] baking dish. Put the vanilla bean seeds and pod, orange juice, and raw sugar in the baking dish. Roast in the oven for 20 minutes, stirring as needed.

Remove the baking dish from the oven and let cool for 30 minutes. Remove the vanilla bean pod from the mixture and discard. Pour the rest of the mixture into the bowl of a food processor (or blender) and pulse until smooth, about 1 minute. Set aside.

**To make the filling:** Place the bittersweet chocolate wafers in a medium heatproof bowl. Set aside.

In a medium saucepan, bring the milk and cream to a boil. Pour the milk mixture over the chocolate and let sit for 5 minutes, then whisk until the chocolate mixture is smooth. Pour the chocolate mixture, butter, and egg into a blender and blend until smooth.

Preheat the oven to 200°F [95°C].

Pour the banana marmalade into the cooled tart shell, spreading it to the edges. Top with the chocolate filling, also spreading it to the edges.

Bake for 20 to 30 minutes, or until the top is set. Let cool at room temperature for about 1 hour.

Remove the chantilly from the refrigerator and beat in a stand mixer fitted with the whisk attachment (or in the bowl in which it was refrigerated, using a hand mixer fitted with the whisk beaters) on low speed until light and airy, about 3 minutes. Spread or pipe the chantilly on the top of the tart. Serve this the same day you make it, because the fillings will make the crust soggy if it sits for longer than 1 day. Store in the refrigerator in a covered cake carrier or wrapped with plastic wrap.

**MAKES ONE 9-IN [23-CM] TART**

# SINFUL CHOCOLATE POUND CAKE

This chocolate pound cake is rich and incredibly moist, with just the flavor of chocolate as your final takeaway.

The secret: Grating a Guittard Nocturne Extra Dark Chocolate Bar (91% cacao) into the cake batter. Our 91 percent chocolate is 52 percent cacao butter, which gives this cake its moist texture. The cake just melts on your tongue. And cacao butter is actually better for you than dairy butter or oil, so while you're enjoying this chocolate cake, you'll have a little twinkle in your eye knowing that the fat in this cake has some health benefits.

One tip before you start: Make sure every ingredient is at room temperature. Too-cold butter will not result in the smooth batter you want.

**CRUMBLE**

½ cup [110 g] unsalted butter, at room temperature

⅔ cup [150 g] Demerara sugar

¾ cup [90 g] cake flour

1 cup [110 g] hazelnuts, toasted (see Note: Toasting Nuts, page 88)

¼ cup [20 g] Guittard Cocoa Rouge (Dutch-processed unsweetened cocoa powder)

¼ tsp baking soda

½ tsp salt

½ tsp ground cinnamon, preferably Saigon cinnamon

## CAKE

1¼ cups [150 g] all-purpose flour

⅓ cup [35 g] Guittard Cocoa Rouge (Dutch-processed unsweetened cocoa powder)

1½ tsp salt

½ tsp baking powder

2 tsp powdered instant coffee

7 Tbsp [100 g] unsalted butter, at room temperature

1½ cups [300 g] granulated sugar

3 large eggs

2 Tbsp water

1 tsp vanilla extract

½ cup plus 1 Tbsp [135 ml] full-fat buttermilk

2 oz [55 g] Guittard Nocturne Extra Dark Chocolate Bar (91% cacao)

**To make the crumble:** Using a food processor, pulse the butter, Demerara sugar, cake flour, hazelnuts, cocoa powder, baking soda, salt, and cinnamon until all the ingredients come together to form a paste, 1 to 2 minutes. Set a strainer or sieve over a large bowl and pour the crumb mixture into the strainer. Lightly press the paste into the strainer to remove any moisture. Transfer the crumble to an airtight container and refrigerate for at least 30 minutes, or up to overnight.

**To make the cake:** Preheat the oven to 350°F [180°C]. Line four 5½-by-3-in [14-by-7.5-cm] or two 9-by-5-in [23-by-12.5-cm] loaf pans with parchment paper along the bottom and up the long sides so extra parchment paper hangs over the sides by about 2 in [5 cm].

In a large bowl, sift together the all-purpose flour, cocoa powder, salt, baking powder, and powdered instant coffee. Set aside.

In the bowl of a stand mixer (or in a large bowl using a hand mixer), beat together the butter and granulated sugar until light and fluffy, about 3 minutes. Beat in the eggs, water, and vanilla until smooth. Add the flour mixture and the buttermilk in alternating additions and beat until smooth, about 2 minutes.

CONTINUED

Using a box grater, grate the chocolate bar. Fold into the batter. Remove the crumble from the refrigerator and sprinkle it over the top of the loaves.

Bake for 30 to 35 minutes, or until a toothpick inserted into the center comes out clean. Let the cakes cool in the loaf pans for 20 minutes. Using the parchment paper, carefully lift the loaves out of the pan and let cool completely on a wire rack. Store, wrapped tightly in plastic wrap, at room temperature for up to 5 days.

**MAKES FOUR 5½-BY-3-IN [14-BY-7.5-CM] LOAVES OR TWO 9-BY-5-IN [23-BY-12.5-CM] LOAVES**

# GRANDMA'S CHOCOLATE CAKE

This cake is rich, moist, and delicious—the kind of chocolate cake you dream about when you're pouring yourself a glass of milk. Donald developed this cake recipe two decades ago when he was the pastry chef for the Four Seasons in Beverly Hills.

As he tells it, "Every hotel pastry chef gets beat up over three things: muffins for the morning breakfast, American-style cookies, and a classic chocolate cake. Sean Loeffel, the food and beverage director at the hotel, had a clear idea of the chocolate cake he wanted me to make. For two months, I made chocolate cakes—every kind of chocolate cake you can imagine—but none of them worked for Sean. Finally, he brought in a cake that his mother had made, and I understood immediately what he wanted (and wished he'd brought in her cake two months earlier).

Sean's mom had 8 or 10 children and a bazillion grandchildren, so she's the grandma that this cake is named for. I tweaked her recipe, using really high-quality chocolate. As soon as I began making it, this cake took off. It became the cake of choice for the many, many weddings held at the Four Seasons. It was the most-requested item for room service. This cake crowns when baked so we would slice off the domed top, save it, and make another dessert—a chocolate pudding cake—by mixing the crumbs of the cutoff tops with a chocolate custard. That dessert also developed a devoted following.

Pastry chef friends from other hotels would call me, complaining about their own chocolate cake trauma, and I would e-mail them this recipe (telling them not to say where they'd gotten it). Without fail, I'd get an e-mail back a few days later singing the praises of this cake."

It's not overstating it to say Donald has made this cake thousands and thousands of times. If you love chocolate cake, this recipe is the one you'll be passing down to your own grandchildren—if they're lucky.

CONTINUED

## CAKE

¾ cup plus 2 Tbsp [210 ml] water

⅓ cup plus 2 Tbsp [55 g] Guittard Cocoa Rouge (Dutch-processed unsweetened cocoa powder)

1¾ cups plus 1 Tbsp [220 g] all-purpose flour

1¾ cups [350 g] sugar

1¼ tsp salt

1 Tbsp baking soda

¾ cup plus 2 Tbsp [210 ml] full-fat buttermilk

½ cup plus 2 Tbsp [150 ml] vegetable oil

2 large eggs

1 tsp vanilla extract

## GANACHE

2⅔ cups [400 g] Guittard Semisweet Chocolate Baking Wafers

1¼ cups [300 ml] heavy whipping cream

2 Tbsp light corn syrup

6 Tbsp [85 g] unsalted butter, at room temperature

## WHITE CHOCOLATE BUTTERCREAM

¾ cup [115 g] Guittard Choc-Au-Lait Baking Chips (white chocolate)

½ cup plus 2 Tbsp [130 g] sugar

3 egg whites, at room temperature

Pinch of salt

¼ tsp vanilla extract

1½ cups [340 g] unsalted butter, cut into ½-in [12-mm] cubes, at room temperature

**To make the cake:** Place a rack in the middle of the oven and preheat the oven to 350°F [180°C]. Butter two 8-in [20-cm] round cake pans.

In a medium saucepan, bring the water to a boil, turn off the heat, and add the cocoa powder. Whisk until smooth, then set aside to cool.

In a large bowl, combine the flour, sugar, salt, and baking soda. With a hand mixer, beat in the buttermilk, vegetable oil, eggs, and vanilla until smooth, about 2 minutes. Add the cocoa mixture and blend until combined, about 30 seconds. Divide the batter between the prepared cake pans and let rest for 30 minutes at room temperature.

Bake for 30 to 35 minutes, or until a toothpick inserted into the center comes out clean. Transfer the cakes to a wire rack to cool for 30 minutes.

Line a baking sheet with parchment paper and sprinkle lightly with sugar.

Using a knife, loosen the sides of the cake. Invert a wire rack over the top of the cake pan, and using both hands, carefully flip the rack and pan together so the pan is upside down on top of the wire rack. Gently shake the pan until the cake falls out, and set the pan aside. Invert a second wire rack on the bottom of the cake and flip back over so it is right-side up. Repeat with the remaining cake layer, and let the cakes cool for about 1 hour. Place the cakes on the prepared baking sheet and refrigerate until the cakes are completely cold, about 1 hour.

**To make the ganache:** Put the semisweet chocolate in a medium heatproof bowl. Set aside.

In a medium saucepan, bring the cream and corn syrup just to a boil. Pour the hot cream mixture over the chocolate. Let the chocolate mixture stand for 3 minutes, then whisk until all of the chocolate has melted. Add the butter and stir until combined. Pour the ganache into a shallow, flat glass baking dish and let cool at room temperature for 1 hour, or until it is spreadable. (At this point, you can wrap the ganache tightly in plastic wrap and store at room temperature for up to 1 day.)

**To make the white chocolate buttercream:** Melt the white chocolate chips using a hot water bath or the microwave oven (see Note: Melting Chocolate, page 51). Stir until completely melted and smooth. Remove the bowl from the water if you used a hot water bath and set aside. Keep the water simmering.

Place the sugar, egg whites, and salt in a second heatproof bowl and set it over the simmering water (creating a second hot water bath). Whisk the sugar mixture continuously until the sugar dissolves and the mixture is very thin and warm, or until a candy thermometer reads 115°F [45°C]. Remove the bowl from the heat and transfer the mixture to the bowl of a stand mixer fitted with the whisk attachment (or to a large bowl if using a hand mixer with whisk beaters). Whisk the sugar mixture on high speed until stiff peaks form, about 5 minutes, then turn the speed to low and mix until cool, about 10 minutes. Add the vanilla and butter on low speed. Add the melted white chocolate in two additions, continuing to blend on low, until combined. Increase the speed to medium and beat until the buttercream is smooth and shiny.

CONTINUED

Using a serrated knife, cut both cakes in half horizontally, for a total of four layers. Place one layer on a cardboard circle or a cake platter. Spread one-third of the ganache on the cake. Carefully place the second cake layer on the ganache and repeat until you have four layers of cake sandwiching three layers of ganache. Refrigerate the cake for 30 minutes.

Apply a "crumb coat" (or first layer) of butter-cream by spreading one-half of the buttercream on the top and sides of the cake. You should be able to see some chocolate crumbs in the white frosting. Chill the cake in the refrigerator for 15 minutes to firm up the buttercream. Use the remaining half of the buttercream to apply the final coat. This time you won't see any choco-late crumbs. It should be completely white. This cake is best eaten the same day it's baked. Store in an airtight container in the refrigerator for up to 1 day.

**MAKES ONE 8-IN [20-CM] TWO-LAYER CAKE**

## CHEF WRESSELL'S TIPS

### - 1 -
Let the cake batter rest for 30 minutes before baking. This allows the leavening to settle down and prevents the fast rise and then fall of the center of the cake in the oven.

### - 2 -
Line two baking sheets with parchment paper and sprinkle with granulated sugar. Place the cooled cake layers on these baking sheets and place them in the refrigerator. The sugar prevents the cake from sticking.

### - 3 -
A "crumb coat," which uses only half of the buttercream, assures that your final frosting will be smooth with no chocolate crumbs showing through.

# CHOCOLATE CARAMELS

Caramel can be daunting the first time you make it. The two things that will help the most when making this recipe are a candy thermometer and a Silpat (silicone) baking mat. Both are easy to find online or in stores that cater to cooks. A candy thermometer will help prevent over-cooking the caramel. If your caramel is slightly undercooked, it'll be soft but that's not a huge problem. You can always refrigerate it to firm it up. If you overcook the caramel, it'll break your teeth! Undercooked is always better than over-cooked. When in doubt, take the pan off the heat. Make sure you have all your ingredients ready and measured out before you start. Once the caramel starts bubbling, the cooking process will happen very quickly and you'll need to keep an eye on the thermometer.

**4½ oz [130 g] Guittard Nocturne Extra Dark Chocolate Bar (91% Cacao), broken into pieces**

**1½ cups [300 g] sugar**

**1 Tbsp plus 1 tsp light corn syrup**

**2 tsp honey**

**⅓ cup [80 ml] water**

**¾ cup [180 ml] heavy whipping cream**

**½ vanilla bean (see Note: Using Vanilla Beans, page 114)**

**¼ tsp baking soda**

**5 Tbsp [65 g] salted butter, at room temperature**

**Fleur de sel for sprinkling**

Oil an 8-by-8-in [20-by-20-cm] cake frame and set it on top of a large piece of parchment paper or Silpat mat on a baking sheet. If you don't have a cake frame, place an 8-by-8-in [20-by-20-cm] piece of parchment paper on top of a sheet of aluminum foil that's about 4 in [10 cm] longer on all four sides. Then roll up the extra foil along the edges of the parchment to form a sort of tray on the Silpat.

Melt the chocolate using a hot water bath or the microwave oven (see Note: Melting Choco-late, page 51). Stir until completely melted and smooth. Remove the bowl from the water if you used a hot water bath and set aside.

CONTINUED

In a large saucepan over high heat, whisk together the sugar, corn syrup, honey, and water.

In a medium saucepan over medium heat, bring the cream, vanilla bean seeds and pod, and baking soda to a boil, stirring frequently, then lower the heat to maintain a simmer.

Stir the sugar mixture to ensure the sugar has dissolved. Continue cooking until the sugar mixture reaches 293°F [145°C] on a candy thermometer. Using a silicone spatula, stir in the butter. Once the butter has completely melted, pour the hot cream mixture into the sugar syrup mixture in two additions, making sure to not break the boil. Stir well until combined. Stir in the melted chocolate. Turn off the heat and keep stirring until the chocolate is completely mixed in, about 2 minutes.

Pour the hot chocolate caramel into the prepared cake frame and sprinkle the fleur de sel over the top. When the caramel has cooled, 1 to 2 hours, remove the frame, or peel back the foil, and transfer the caramel to a cutting board. (If your caramels are still too sticky to cut, refrigerate for 30 minutes to 1 hour.) Cut the caramels into the desired shapes and wrap with plastic wrap, wax paper, or candy wrappers. Store individually wrapped caramels in a cool place for up to 1 month.

**MAKES ABOUT FORTY CARAMELS, DEPENDING ON SIZE**

# CHOCOLATE MARSHMALLOWS

Homemade marshmallows have a texture that is lighter and at the same time more satisfying than store-bought marshmallows. This recipe is elevated by high-quality chocolate. Using a stand mixer to make these will make it easier to juggle stirring and pouring a boiling mixture at the same time. A candy thermometer is a smart investment, as it will help with precision.

Other than eating them or putting them in hot cocoa, the best part of making marshmallows is flavoring them. Rather than the traditional dredging mixture of confectioners' sugar and cornstarch, Donald likes to dredge the marshmallows in a mixture of cocoa powder and confectioners' sugar, sifted together. You can add finely ground spices or flavorings to the mix—cardamom, cinnamon, nutmeg, instant coffee, or even a little salt—to make your marshmallows stand out.

5 oz [140 g] Guittard Bittersweet Chocolate Baking Bars, broken into small pieces, or Wafers

⅔ cup [160 ml] warm water

2 Tbsp unflavored powdered gelatin

1 cup plus 2 Tbsp [230 g] granulated sugar

¼ cup [80 g] honey

⅓ cup [80 ml] light corn syrup

¼ cup [20 g] Guittard Cocoa Rouge (Dutch-processed unsweetened cocoa powder)

¼ cup [30 g] confectioners' sugar

Oil an 8-by-8-in [20-by-20-cm] cake frame and set it on top of a large piece of parchment paper or Silpat mat on a baking sheet. If you don't have a cake frame, place an 8-by-8-in [20-by-20-cm] piece of parchment paper on top of a sheet of aluminum foil that's about 4 in [10 cm] longer on all four sides. Then roll up the extra foil along the edges of the parchment to form a sort of tray on the Silpat. Oil an additional sheet of parchment paper and set aside.

Melt the chocolate using a hot water bath or the microwave oven (see Note: Melting Chocolate, page 51). Stir until completely melted and smooth. Remove the bowl from the water if you used a hot water bath and set aside.

In a shallow bowl, pour in ⅓ cup [80 ml] of the warm water and sprinkle the gelatin over the surface. Let the gelatin absorb the water for 5 to 10 minutes. Then pour the hydrated gelatin into the bowl of a stand mixer fitted with the whisk attachment (or into a large bowl, and fit a hand mixer with whisk beaters).

In a large saucepan, combine the granulated sugar, honey, and remaining ⅓ cup [80 ml] warm water and heat until the mixture reaches 230°F [110°C] on a candy thermometer.

With the mixer running, pour the corn syrup into the hydrated gelatin and beat together. Set the mixer to medium-high speed and slowly pour in the hot sugar mixture. Beat until white and frothy. It's done when a candy thermometer reads 115°F [45°C]. Fold in the melted chocolate until just combined.

Pour the marshmallow mixture into the prepared cake frame and cover with the oiled parchment paper. Let the marshmallow rest at room temperature for 4 hours, or overnight.

Sift the cocoa powder and confectioners' sugar together into a shallow bowl. Set aside.

Remove the marshmallow from the parchment paper on the baking sheet and set it on a clean cutting board. Peel the parchment paper from the marshmallow and cut the marshmallow into cubes. (If they stick to the knife, sprinkle them with some of the cocoa-sugar mixture as you cut.) Toss the cubes in the cocoa-sugar mixture. Store in an airtight container at room temperature for up to 1 week.

**MAKES SIXTY-FOUR 1-IN [2.5-CM] MARSHMALLOWS**

*Chapter 7*

# TOPPINGS

---

hot fudge topping

whipped cream

salted caramel

*buttercream frosting*

*chocolate ganache*

*chocolate shell*

*chocolate crème fraîche frosting*

# HOT FUDGE TOPPING

My grandmother had to force dessert on us. I know this doesn't earn me much sympathy. She would fill us to the brim with meat loaf and mashed potatoes, urging us to clean our plates, only to proclaim that she had dessert waiting on the sidelines. Aside from eclairs, her favorite dessert was ice cream with hot fudge topping. Just chocolate, nothing else. While I always hoped she might surprise us with a maraschino cherry, she never did. Decades later, I realize she was right. Deep, intense, thick, and creamy at the same time, my granny's hot fudge topping is the only thing ice cream needs. Drizzle it over ice cream, cookies, pies, or eat it straight from a spoon.

**5 oz [140 g] Guittard Semisweet Chocolate Baking Bars, broken into pieces**

**¼ cup [55 g] unsalted butter, at room temperature**

**⅓ cup [75 ml] whole milk**

**½ cup [50 g] sifted confectioners' sugar**

**1 Tbsp Guittard Cocoa Rouge (Dutch-processed unsweetened cocoa powder)**

**1 tsp vanilla extract, or 1 Tbsp Kahlúa, Grand Marnier, or other liqueur**

Melt the chocolate and butter together using a hot water bath or the microwave oven (see Note: Melting Chocolate, page 51). Stir until completely melted and smooth. Remove the bowl from the water if you used a hot water bath.

Whisk the milk, confectioners' sugar, cocoa powder, and vanilla into the chocolate mixture until completely smooth. Store in the refrigerator in an airtight container for up to 1 week.

When you're ready to use the topping, reheat in the microwave on medium until warm and smooth, about 30 seconds.

**MAKES 1¼ CUPS [280 G]**

# CHOCOLATE GANACHE

My first experience making ganache was a nightmare. Mind you, I have a tendency to skip reading recipe directions and assume I'll just figure it out as I go along. I had high hopes that melting a bag of our semisweet chocolate chips and folding in some warm-ish cream would yield the perfect ganache that I had seen our chefs make countless times. I was so wrong. My ganache turned into a congealed, anything-but-emulsified glob. Here are a few helpful tips from the best chefs I know (tips given to me only after I promised to carefully follow their directions): It's all about the right chocolate (one with a lower fat content works best!), proportions (chocolate to dairy), and the finer details (timing and temperature), which you'll find explained in this recipe. In fact, chocolate and cream form the perfect union that, when mastered, results in a decadent texture.

**4 oz [115 g] Guittard Bittersweet or Semisweet Chocolate Baking Bars, broken into small pieces**

**½ cup [120 ml] heavy whipping cream**

Place the chocolate in a medium heatproof bowl.

In a medium saucepan over medium heat, heat the cream until bubbles start to form around the edges. Pour the hot cream over the chocolate and let sit for 2 minutes. Using a clean, dry, silicone spatula, stir to combine until all of the chocolate is melted and the mixture is smooth. Let the ganache cool, about 15 minutes. Store wrapped tightly in plastic wrap in the refrigerator for up to 1 week.

When you're ready to use the ganache, let it sit at room temperature for 15 minutes. Reheat the ganache in a microwave in 20-second intervals and stir with a clean, dry spatula after each interval until it's smooth. Let cool to room temperature, about 5 minutes.

**MAKES ABOUT 1 CUP [225 G]**

**NOTE:** RESCUING GANACHE. Sometimes the proportions of the cream and chocolate are off, other times the temperatures are too hot or cold. But most of the time, broken ganache happens when it's not stirred properly. If you see the ganache start to separate and look grainy, put a little bit of cold heavy cream in a bowl. With a whisk in one hand, ladle a bit of the ganache into the cold cream and whisk it in a figure-eight pattern, integrating the cream until the ganache comes back together and returns to its characteristic shiny appearance. Add the remaining ganache and whisk to blend well.

# CHOCOLATE SHELL

I love a thin shell of good chocolate over ice cream. Pour this on ice cream and it hardens within seconds. Like butter, coconut oil has a high melting point, so it melts easily but then hardens quickly once it gets cold.

**1 cup [150 g] Guittard Bittersweet Chocolate Baking Wafers**

**1 Tbsp coconut oil**

Melt the chocolate and coconut oil together using a hot water bath or the microwave oven (see Note: Melting Chocolate, page 51). Stir until completely melted and smooth. Remove the bowl from the water if you used a hot water bath and set aside to cool, about 20 minutes. Store in a jar at room temperature for up to 1 week. If the shell hardens, reheat in the microwave in 20-second intervals and swirl the shell in the jar after each interval until it's easy to pour. Let the shell cool to room temperature before using, about 5 minutes.

**MAKES ⅔ CUP [165 ML]**

# SALTED CARAMEL

Salted caramel is kind of an overachiever. And I say that with love. Why? Because it's good at pretty much everything. It's good at salt. It's good at sweet. It's good at chewy. It's great as a confection, an ice cream flavor, a sauce for ice cream, and even a filling. Here we're calling it a topping, but you can try this as a layer in Jim's Special Fudge (page 131) or fill cupcakes with it.

**⅔ cup [130 g] superfine sugar**
**½ cup [120 ml] heavy whipping cream**
**1 tsp fleur de sel**

Pour ⅓ cup [65 g] of the sugar into a medium saucepan over medium heat. Swirl the saucepan around as the sugar starts to melt. Do not use a spoon or spatula at this point. When the sugar is almost melted, add the remaining ⅓ cup [65 g] sugar and swirl the saucepan until all of the sugar is melted. Slowly and carefully add the cream. The caramel will bubble up. Add the fleur de sel and continue to cook over medium heat until a candy thermometer reads 225°F [110°C], or the sauce has turned medium brown. Remove from the heat and let cool for 5 to 10 minutes. Store in an airtight container in the refrigerator for up to 2 weeks.

When you're ready to use the caramel, let it sit at room temperature for 1 hour. Pour the sauce into a saucepan and reheat over medium heat until warm, 2 to 5 minutes.

**MAKES ¾ CUP [135 G]**

# CHOCOLATE CRÈME FRAÎCHE FROSTING

This is my go-to recipe when I want a not-too-sweet finish for a rich dessert like Flourless Chocolate Cake (page 94) or a sweet breakfast treat like Chocolate Cherry Scones (page 31). For this frosting, I like to add a little extra flavor by scraping out the seeds of a vanilla bean instead of using vanilla extract.

**1 cup [240 ml] crème fraîche or sour cream**

**Seeds from 1 vanilla bean (see Note: Using Vanilla Beans, page 114), or ½ tsp vanilla extract**

**2 Tbsp sugar**

**1 Tbsp Guittard Cocoa Rouge (Dutch-processed unsweetened cocoa powder)**

In the bowl of a stand mixer fitted with a whisk attachment (or in a medium bowl using a hand mixer fitted with whisk beaters), beat together the crème fraîche, vanilla bean seeds, sugar, and cocoa powder until thickened and smooth, 20 to 30 seconds. Be careful not to overbeat. Store in an airtight container in the refrigerator for up to 3 days.

When you're ready to use the frosting, let it sit at room temperature for 30 minutes. Whisk using a stand mixer with the whisk attachment (or in a large bowl using a hand mixer with whisk beaters) for 1 minute, or until smooth and fluffy.

**MAKES 1 CUP [230 G]**

# BUTTERCREAM FROSTING

This is my favorite frosting and it's very simple—just milk, butter, and sugar, plus a bit of nostalgia. This frosting will take you back to your favorite cakes from childhood. Basic and versatile, this recipe can be modified by adding any flavor you like: lemon zest, espresso, lavender, or even rosewater. The trick with flavoring is to add 1 tsp, taste, and then add more if you wish.

**1 cup [220 g] unsalted butter, at room temperature**

**2⅔ cups [320 g] confectioners' sugar**

**1 Tbsp plus 1 tsp whole milk**

**2 tsp vanilla extract**

In the bowl of a stand mixer fitted with a whisk attachment (or in a medium bowl using a hand mixer fitted with whisk beaters), beat together the butter, confectioners' sugar, milk, and vanilla until thickened and smooth. Store in an airtight container in the refrigerator for up to 4 days.

When you're ready to use the frosting, let it sit at room temperature for 30 minutes. Whisk using a stand mixer with the whisk attachment (or in a large bowl using a hand mixer with whisk beaters) for 1 minute, or until smooth and fluffy.

**MAKES 2 CUPS [410 G]**

# WHIPPED CREAM

Homemade whipped cream is easy to make and will blow the socks off anyone used to the stuff that comes in a tub out of your supermarket freezer. It also epitomizes one of those miraculous kitchen transformations that never gets old. Just remember to start using your mixer on low speed so you don't splash yourself before the cream turns into soft peaks. Increase the speed as the peaks begin to form, and don't overwhip. My mom used to add a dash of vanilla extract, so feel free to do that or get even more creative by adding liqueur, bitters, lemon zest, or spices.

**1 cup [240 ml] heavy whipping cream, chilled**

**2 Tbsp superfine sugar**

**1 Tbsp liqueur (coffee, chocolate, orange, Kahlúa), 1 Tbsp minced citrus zest (lemon, lime, or orange), 1 tsp flavored bitters (strawberry, rhubarb, ginger), or 2 tsp other flavorings (espresso powder, cocoa powder, hot chocolate mix, or cinnamon) of your choice**

In the bowl of a stand mixer fitted with the chilled whisk attachment (or in a chilled medium bowl with a hand mixer fitted with chilled whisk beaters), beat together the cream and sugar until soft peaks form, about 3 minutes. Add any liqueur or flavoring to the whipped cream right after you see soft peaks form. Whip for 1 minute to ensure that your addition doesn't cause the cream to fall. Store tightly covered with plastic wrap in the refrigerator for up to 3 days. When you're ready to use the whipped cream, let it sit at room temperature for 20 minutes. Whip using a stand mixer with the whisk attachment (or in a large bowl using a hand mixer with whisk beaters) for 1 minute, or until fluffy.

**MAKES 2 CUPS [480 ML]**

# *Acknowledgments*

This book represents a labor of love for one hundred forty-seven years and five generations of Guittards. I'm merely the storyteller, the one who couldn't help but raise her hand to receive the memories, flavors, and kitchen adventures so they could be committed to paper.

A cookbook is not only produced but also celebrated by community. This book would not be possible without the traditions that came before me and the extended family of farmers, employees, customers, and chocolate lovers (that's you!) who inspire us every day to be a better company and make better chocolate. I'm baking an imaginary chocolate cake for everyone who believed that this project could become more than I would have ever envisioned.

Thanks to my tremendous team at Chronicle Books, who decided to take me under their wing to make this book a reality, including Sarah Billingsley for her editing prowess, vision, and guidance and Lorena Jones for taking it to the finish line; Vanessa Dina, for designing a beautiful book that celebrates our heritage, honors our brand, and tells our story (not to mention for her ability to put together a killer playlist to get us through a marathon photo shoot amidst a heat wave); photographer Antonis Achilleos and stylists Lillian Kang and Christine Wolheim, and their dream teams, who showed our chocolate and our recipes so much TLC; managing editor Doug Ogan, who made so many passes through this book; production developer Tera Killip and production designer Steve Kim, who made sure it was perfectly printed; marketing manager (and biggest fan of chocolate and chocolate wrappers around) Peter Perez; and publicist David Hawk for being as excited to tell our story as we are.

Thanks to:
My editing team Amanda Poulsen Dix and Ann Spivack. Amanda was at my side for the entirety of this project as my recipe tester, taste tester, and cheerleader, rightfully earning the title of Queen of the Test Kitchen. She is the only one patient enough to sit and ponder my indecisive wordsmithing and steadfast enough to make sure that a recipe works in whatever kitchen, whatever oven, whatever pan. Her knowledge, enthusiasm, and determination made this book. Thank goodness we ran into each other at that Giants game (and big thanks to Stephen for ensuring I pressed "send"). Ann lent me her keen copy-editor's eye and swift and honest feedback, keeping my storytelling on point.

Alice Medrich, for her collaboration, support, and inspiration and for so gracefully introducing this book.

Deborah Kwan, for lending an ear and an eye for the concept in the earliest of stages and for her friendship and lighthearted perspective during the craziest of times.

Guittard pastry chef Donald Wressell for his creativity, brainiac pastry and chocolate knowledge, letting me drive his truck, and for his willingness to contribute masterpieces and pro tips to this project.

My honorary uncles, Gerry, Mark and Ed, for their inspiring commitment to our family business and for a commendable recall of some of these recipes and the people behind them. I'm like a sponge trying to soak up all of their collective knowledge. I can always count on the three of them for honest feedback and steadfast and unwavering support and encouragement.

Frina for all the years of service and passion, the hugs, the laughter, and for the recipe-enhancing tidbit she gave me in her kitchen that one Saturday afternoon.

Micki and Thalia for entertaining my kitchen curiosity during summer vacations spent at the factory.

The entire family of Guittard employees for all the hard work, dedication, and passion, and to everyone, past and present, who is behind the magic of these recipes.

My dear friend, Yigit Pura, for making me laugh, keeping me on my toes, and always, always reminding me to be on the lookout for unicorns.

Katie K, for being my best audience.

Last but never least, closing thanks and affection go to my ever-loving mama, Lyn, whose character cannot be qualified by any one adjective; my brother, Jesse, for his inspiration, goofiness, and constant reminders to dream big; and my dad/boss, Gary, for leading this company with a vengeance, holding true to our heritage and the traditions that have made us who we are, yet constantly pushing forward to make sure we're always thinking beyond our wildest chocolate dreams. I never really thought about what it would be like to come to work every day and sit fifteen feet from my dad. Turns out, it's pretty great.

# Index

ittard GUITTARD Guittard's Guittard GUITTARD Guittard
ittard GUITTARD MFG. CO. Guittard Guittard GUITTARD MFG. CO. Guittar

ittard GUITTARD Guittard's Guittard GUITTARD Guittard
ittard GUITTARD MFG. CO. Guittard Guittard GUITTARD MFG. CO. Guittar

ittard GUITTARD Guittard's Guittard GUITTARD Guittard
ittard GUITTARD MFG. CO. Guittard Guittard GUITTARD MFG. CO. Guittar

ittard GUITTARD Guittard's Guittard GUITTARD Guittard
ittard GUITTARD MFG. CO. Guittard Guittard GUITTARD MFG. CO. Guittar

ittard GUITTARD Guittard's Guittard GUITTARD Guittard
ittard GUITTARD MFG. CO. Guittard Guittard GUITTARD MFG. CO. Guittar

ittard GUITTARD Guittard's Guittard GUITTARD Guittard
ittard GUITTARD MFG. CO. Guittard Guittard GUITTARD MFG. CO. Guittar

ittard GUITTARD Guittard's Guittard GUITTARD Guittard
ittard GUITTARD MFG. CO. Guittard Guittard GUITTARD MFG. CO. Guittar

ittard GUITTARD Guittard's Guittard GUITTARD Guittard
ittard GUITTARD MFG. CO. Guittard Guittard GUITTARD MFG. CO. Guittar

ittard GUITTARD Guittard's Guittard GUITTARD Guittard
ittard GUITTARD MFG. CO. Guittard Guittard GUITTARD MFG. CO. Guittar